BTEC Level 2 First Study Skills Guide in Public Services

Welcome to your Study Skills Guide! You can make it your own – start by adding your personal and course details below...

Learner's name:

BTEC course title:

Date started:

Mandatory units:

Optional units:

Centre name:

Centre address:

Tutor's name:

Published by Pearson Education Limited, a company incorporated in England and Wales, having its registered office at Edinburgh Gate, Harlow, Essex, CM20 2JE. Registered company number: 872828

Edexcel is a registered trademark of Edexcel Limited

Text © Pearson Education Limited 2010

First published 2010

13 12
10 9 8 7 6

British Library Cataloguing in Publication Data
A catalogue record for this book is available from the British Library

ISBN 978 1 84690 571 1

Typeset and edited by Sparks Publishing Services Ltd
Cover design by Visual Philosophy, created by eMC Design
Cover photo/illustration © Getty Images: The Image Bank/Derek Berwin
Printed in Great Britain by Ashford Colour Press Ltd

Acknowledgements

The author and publisher would like to thank the following individuals and organisations for permission to reproduce photographs:

Alamy Images: Mark Harvey 41, Ace Stock Limited 60, Jacky Chapman, Janine Wiedel Photolibrary 14; **Corbis:** 65, Comstock 5; **Getty Images:** Nicolas Asfouri / AFP 46; **Pearson Education Ltd:** Steve Shott 26, Ian Wedgewood 37; **TopFoto:** John Powell 22

Cover images: *Front:* **Getty Images:** Derek Berwin / The Image Bank

All other images © Pearson Education

Every effort has been made to contact copyright holders of material reproduced in this book. Any omissions will be rectified in subsequent printings if notice is given to the publishers.

Websites

Go to www.pearsonhotlinks.co.uk to gain access to the relevant website links and information on how they can aid your studies. When you access the site, search for either the title BTEC Level 2 First Study Skills Guide in Public Services or ISBN 9781846905711.

Disclaimer

This material has been published on behalf of Edexcel and offers high-quality support for the delivery of Edexcel qualifications.
This does not mean that the material is essential to achieve any Edexcel qualification, nor does it mean that it is the only suitable material available to support any Edexcel qualification. Edexcel material will not be used verbatim in setting any Edexcel examination or assessment. Any resource lists produced by Edexcel shall include this and other appropriate resources. Copies of official specifications for all Edexcel qualifications may be found on the Edexcel website: www.edexcel.com

Contents

Popular progression pathways

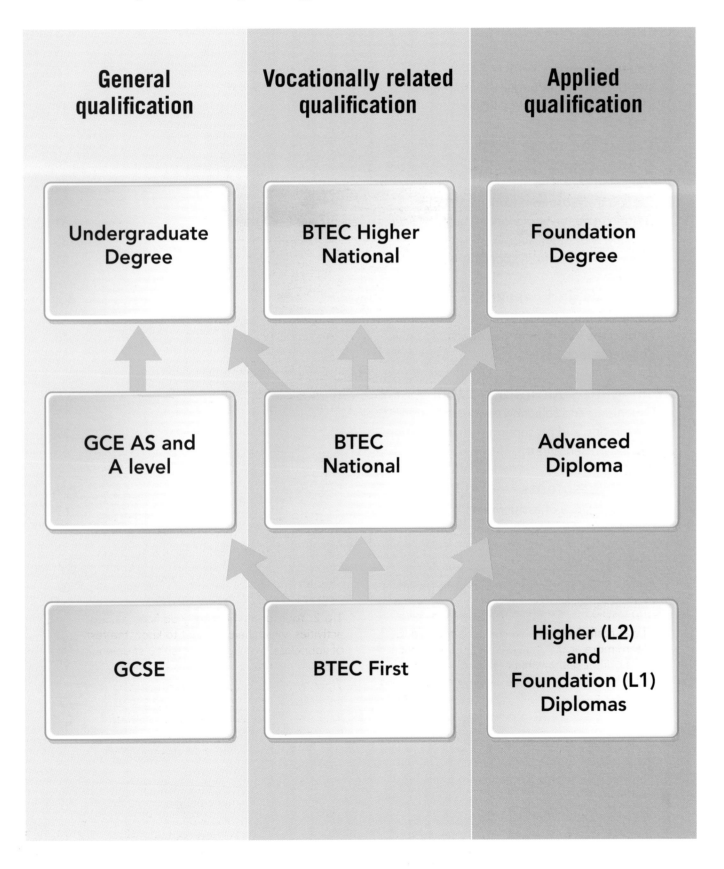

Your BTEC First course
Early days

Every year many new learners start BTEC Level 2 First courses, enjoy the challenge and successfully achieve their award. Some do this the easy way; others make it harder for themselves.

Everyone will have different feelings when they start their course.

Case study: Your BTEC Level 2 First course

Halima has been accepted onto a BTEC Level 2 First in Public Services course starting in September.

'My careers adviser at school said that we needed to apply really early for a public services course because they are really popular and fill up fast so I did as she said and applied early.

I was really looking forward to being able to learn more about the services and the police in particular as my ultimate goal is to apply for the Police Service. I think I would make a good police officer and would be proud to represent my community.

Although I wasn't nervous at my interview I'm starting to get really nervous now. I've been to the same school for the last five years and moving to a centre with new people and new tutors is quite scary.

I had a chat with my mum about it and she suggested we go to see the BTEC First course tutor and discuss my concerns so I'm not quite so nervous when I start the course. The tutor was really understanding. She said that everyone feels the same way when they are starting something new, and she gave me some really good tips about how to relax and enjoy the first couple of weeks on the course.

- **Tip 1:** Remember everyone is feeling just as nervous as you are. This means you already have something in common with all the other people on your course.

- **Tip 2:** Your tutors will usually do 'icebreaking' activities, which help you get to know the rest of your class. Making friends isn't just down to you – the tutors will help you as well.

- **Tip 3:** Remember you wouldn't have been accepted on the course if the tutors who interviewed you didn't think you could do the work. Although you may have to manage your time carefully and plan properly, you **can** do the work.

- **Tip 4:** Remember your tutors are there to support you. If you have any problems they will be happy to help and guide you.

I felt much better after speaking to her and although I'm still a bit nervous about my first day, the tips she gave me helped give me a bit more confidence to face my fears and overcome them.'

About your course

What do you know already?

If someone asks you about your course, could you give a short, accurate description? If you can, you have a good understanding of what your course is about. This has several benefits.

Four benefits of understanding your course

1 You will be better prepared and organised.

2 You can make links between the course and the world around you.

3 You can check how your personal interests and hobbies relate to the course.

4 You will be alert to information that relates to topics you are studying, whether it's from conversations with family and friends, watching television or at a part-time job.

Read any information you have been given by your centre. You can also check the Edexcel website for further details – go to www.edexcel.com.

Interest/hobby	How this relates to my studies

What else do you need to know?

Five facts you should find out about your course

1. The type of BTEC qualification you are studying.
2. How many credits your qualification is worth.
3. The number of mandatory units you will study and what they cover.
4. How many credits the mandatory units are worth.
5. The number of optional units you need to study in total and the options available in your centre.

BTEC FACT

BTEC First Certificate = 15 credits

BTEC First Extended Certificate = 30 credits

BTEC First Diploma = 60 credits

Generally, the more credits there are, the longer it takes to study for the qualification.

Case study: How does the course work?

Sam and India are twins who both want a career in the public services. Sam is interested in being a probation officer while India really wants to be a prison officer. They have both been told by their careers adviser that the BTEC Level 2 First Diploma in Public Services might be a good choice for them, but after discussing it they can't understand how one course can help both of them when they want such different careers. They decide to do some research to find out how the course will be best for both of them.

Sam makes an appointment to speak with the careers adviser and finds out that the BTEC Level 2 First Diploma is designed to help people who want a career in any public service, not just a specific service. It deals with the general skills and knowledge you need across all the services, which can be really helpful if you change your mind about the service you want to join.

India makes an appointment to see the public services tutor at the local further education college and finds out that the BTEC First Diploma is worth 60 credits and is made up of six different units:

- three Mandatory units (you have to take these) for 25 credits
- one Optional Specialist unit (you can choose one of two units) for 5 credits
- a number of Optional units (you can choose from the selection of units offered by your centre) to make up the remaining 30 credits.

This means that you can choose to take units that suit your interests and your possible choice of career for the future. India also learns that a BTEC Level 2 First Diploma course can last anything from one to three years, depending on how your centre chooses to run the course and which other subjects you pair it with.

The twins meet up after their research and compare what they found out. They discover that:

1. The BTEC First in Public Services is really useful for any service.
2. It provides you with lots of different skills and abilities that you can take to any job.
3. It has six units: three mandatory, one Optional Specialist and a choice of various Optional units, which means that there is scope to tailor the course to suit you.
4. You can do it over one, two or three years, depending on how the course is run by your centre and whether you want to pair it with other qualifications, such as some extra GCSEs.

The twins realise that the course could actually be suitable for both of them, although they may consider taking different combinations of the Optional Specialist and Optional units offered by their centre.

Activity: How well do you know your course?

Complete this activity to check that you know the main facts. Compare your answers with a friend. You should have similar answers except where you make personal choices, such as about optional units. Your tutor can help you complete number 9.

1 The correct title of the BTEC award I am studying is:

2 The length of time it will take me to complete my award is:

3 The number of mandatory units I have to study is:

4 The titles of my mandatory units, and their credit values, are:

5 The main topics I will learn in each mandatory unit include:

Mandatory unit	Main topics

6 The number of credits I need to achieve by studying optional units is:

7 The titles of my optional units, and their credit values, are:

8 The main topics I will learn in each optional unit include:

Optional unit	Main topics

9 Other important aspects of my course are:

10 After I have achieved my BTEC First, my options include:

Introduction to the public services sector

The public services sector is a huge area of employment. Hundreds of different organisations make up the public sector and there are thousands of job roles within these organisations.

Look around your area and consider what our public services do for us. Who do you go to if you are ill? Who do you call in an emergency? Who organises your local sports facilities or pool? Who runs your local library? What would you do if you had your mobile phone or wallet stolen? Without the public services our lives would be very different.

It is important to remember that public services are not just the emergency and armed services. These are the most visible services but there are a huge number of people working behind the scenes in a great variety of roles to provide essential services that we often take for granted.

In the event of a major incident such as a terrorist bombing or severe flooding the public services work together to protect lives and property. Listed below are some of the services that could be involved in a terrorist incident. Can you think of any more? Add your ideas to the list.

Police Service
Firefighters
Paramedics
Territorial Army
Local council
Victim Support

Did you realise how many different services might work together to help the public?

Do any of these jobs appeal to you?

Generally the public services are considered to fall into two categories: uniformed and non-uniformed. The table below shows examples of these.

Uniformed	Non-uniformed
Police Service	Probation Service
Fire and Rescue Service	Social Services
Prison Service	Education Service
HM Coastguard	Local Government
Royal Navy	Youth and Community Services
Royal Air Force	Intelligence Services
National Health Service	Mountain Rescue
Ambulance Service	The Courts Service
British Transport Police	

The interesting thing is that many services can fall into more than one category, for example most nurses wear uniform but many doctors do not. Mountain and Cave Rescue workers may not wear a uniform but sometimes have to perform similar rescue work to the Fire Service.

These days all the organisations listed above work together closely. This is called a 'multi-agency approach' and it is important for the success of the services. No single service can tackle society's problems on its own, which is why working in partnership is such a good idea. It means the services can share their knowledge and resources to combat the biggest problems affecting the public.

The uniformed and non-uniformed public services work together to help solve some of the most pressing problems in society. In your opinion what are the social problems the public want the services to deal with as a priority?

Case study: Working in the public services

Qassim completed his BTEC First in Public Services in 2002 and now works as a police officer on a safer neighbourhood team in an inner city area.

'When I was younger I didn't want to be a police officer. I thought I would be a professional footballer – I think most young lads think that before they realise what they really want to do.

I was 15 and in my last year of school when a good friend of mine died in a stabbing incident. I was devastated and the impact on his family was enormous – they never really got over it. One thing that sticks in my mind about that time was the professionalism and attitude of the police officers who helped and supported us through it. I knew from that point on I wanted to be a police officer to try and educate young people about carrying knives and maybe save other people from the heartache I saw my friends and family go through.

I did a BTEC Level 2 First in Public Services at a local college and then went straight on to do the BTEC Level 3 National. I really enjoyed the crime and justice units so I then applied to university to do a degree in Law and Criminology. I started applying for the Police Service in my last year at university and, after some really hard interviews and tests, I was lucky enough to be accepted.

Being a police officer in an inner city area means every day is a challenge. The problems faced by the communities – such as gang issues, drugs and car crime – can't be solved in a day but I wouldn't change my job for anything. Every day my job makes a difference to people's lives and this makes it all worthwhile for me.'

Skills you need for your sector

A variety of skills are needed to be successful in the public service sector, some of which you may already have while others can be difficult to learn. A BTEC Level 2 First in Public Services will help you enhance the skills you already have and develop those you aren't quite so good at yet.

Communication skills

- **Verbal communication**

  In the public services you will be in constant verbal communication with colleagues, superiors, members of the public and other services. It is essential that your tone and clarity of speech is good. You may need to project your voice to a crowd or speak softly to a victim of crime; you may need to speak firmly and confidently to a rowdy gang or very clearly to someone who is hard of hearing. The skill is choosing which type of verbal communication is appropriate for each situation, as choosing the wrong type could lead to a situation becoming worse instead of better.

Non-verbal communication

Your body language can tell another person a great deal about you. In fact it is estimated that about 80 per cent of all the information we receive from another person comes from their body language rather than their speech. Controlling your body language and thinking about gesture, facial expressions, posture and use of eye contact are essential skills for those working in the public sector. For example, an army officer must show confident body language when leading a mission or the team might lose confidence in their ability.

Listening

This is a vital skill across all public services. You need to listen to the instructions you are given, and you need to listen to what the public may have to say to you so you are able to act on the information you receive. If you are taking a statement from someone you will have to ask the right questions but, perhaps even more importantly, you will also have to listen very carefully to the answers. You may think you already know how to listen, but how many times have you interrupted someone while they were speaking or misunderstood instructions you have been given? The public services require 'active listeners'. This can be summarised as listening with a purpose. It involves paying attention to what is being said and questioning the speaker to ensure real understanding has been achieved. Active listening requires as much energy as speaking and it is a skill that requires practice and development if it is to be perfected. Many potential public service recruits need to improve this skill.

Written communication and reading

Although the public services may look very glamorous on TV, the reality is that some of your time will be taken up with paperwork and reading documents. This part of the job may involve writing emails, internal memos and reports, taking notes, and skimming, scanning or reading documents in detail. These tasks require you to have a good standard of written English and to be able to read fluently. Many of the services use reading and writing tests as part of their interview processes, so improving these skills is essential.

Your BTEC course will help you develop all-round skills, like communication.

Teamwork

- **Cooperation**

  You will be working alongside individuals of all ages, races, religions and nationalities. You must be able to work in cooperation with all of these different people if you are going to be successful. Can you leave your prejudices behind? What if you had a personality clash with a colleague – could you still work with them successfully? Public service cooperation is called 'collaborative working'. It is very important because uniformed and non-uniformed services have to work together on a variety of tasks such as major incident response and child protection.

- **Leadership**

  There may be times you are placed into a leadership position, particularly as your career progresses. Leadership is not an easy skill to learn – it requires confidence and knowledge. Good leaders can make the difference between the success and failure of a team so this skill is very important to the public services.

- **Problem solving**

  Problem-solving abilities are essential in any job role, but they are particularly important to the public services. Many primary roles involve solving problems, such as how to move a casualty to hospital, how to stop a prison riot, where to house refugees or how to solve a crime.

- **Commitment**

  You must be able to demonstrate commitment and dedication both to join the services in the first place and to ensure you stay in the sector. Service work is challenging and often exhausting. It is not a job you can do with a half-hearted attitude: you must be prepared to work long hours and do difficult tasks.

Personal skills

- **Discipline**

  Discipline in the public services is very different from the kind of discipline you may face in other careers. Self-discipline is a really useful skill; this is where you are able to monitor and control your own conduct and behaviour. You will also need to be disciplined in your timekeeping. The way you present yourself, including the pride you take in your appearance, is also key. The public services demand high standards of personal conduct so if this isn't a strength of yours it might be time to consider improving it.

- **Fitness**

  Fitness is really important as most uniformed public services have a physical fitness test that you have to pass to get a job. Also being physically fit helps you cope with the stress and pressure you will come under during your day-to-day work. The BTEC Level 2 First Diploma has a fitness unit built in as a core element of the course.

- **Decision making**

  The nature of public service work means that sometimes you have to make on-the-spot decisions. The Public Service Skills unit of your course will help you develop this skill.

○ **Risk assessment**

Firefighters don't rush into a burning building, police officers don't immediately remove victims from car accidents and the armed services do not rush into conflict. They assess the situation first. An injured firefighter can't save anyone! The skill of assessing the risk before you act is essential in service life.

○ **Compassion**

Many people think the services are a macho environment, but this has changed significantly over the last 20 years. You may be dealing with the most vulnerable sections of society – people who are injured, scared, unable to communicate or have lost a loved one. You will need to treat such people with kindness and compassion.

○ **Trustworthiness**

This is a key aspect of the public services. The public must be able to trust you, quite possibly with their lives, and the lives of your colleagues may also be in your hands.

○ **Reliability**

Being reliable means ensuring you are where you are supposed to be, when you are supposed to be there, doing exactly what you are supposed to do. In an emergency service call-out, if you don't get to the location on time, lives or property might be at risk.

○ **Courage**

Some of the situations faced by the emergency and armed services will draw on all your courage. Facing the unexpected and dealing with it successfully on your course will help you learn this ability.

Regardless of the public services career you want to join there are some essential **personal, learning and thinking skills (PLTS)** that you will develop while you are completing your BTEC programme. See page 87 for more information on these.

More about BTEC Level 2 Firsts

What is different about a BTEC Level 2 First?

How you learn

Expect to be 'hands-on'. BTEC Level 2 Firsts are practical and focus on the skills and knowledge needed in the workplace. You will learn new things and learn how to apply your knowledge.

BTEC First learners are expected to take responsibility for their own learning and be keen and well-organised. You should enjoy having more freedom, while knowing you can still ask for help or support if you need it.

How you are assessed

Many BTEC First courses are completed in one year, but if you are taking GCSEs as well, you may be doing it over two years or more. You will be assessed by completing **assignments** written by your tutors. These are based on **learning outcomes** set by Edexcel. Each assignment will have a deadline.

Which of your units or assignments do you think will be the most challenging?

TOP TIPS

You can use your Study Skills Guide with the Edexcel Student Book for BTEC Level 2 First Public Services (Edexcel, 2010). It includes the main knowledge you'll need, with tips from BTEC experts, Edexcel assignment tips, assessment activities and up-to-date case studies from industry experts, plus handy references to your Study Skills Guide.

Case study: Completing assignments

Genevieve looks back at the assignments she completed in her first year on the BTEC Level 2 First Diploma in Public Services.

'This year has been really interesting for me because I am doing the Diploma alongside five GCSEs at school, and the assessments can be quite different. So far I've completed assignments on three units: Public Service Skills, Sport and Recreation in the Public Services, and Crime and Its Effects on Society.

My favourite assignment so far was for the Crime unit. We had to work individually to produce a poster on the role of a crime scene investigator. I liked the assignment because it was a really different topic from my GCSEs and I was able to be more independent with my research. I spent some time looking up the role of the crime scene team in the library and on the Internet, but what really made the assignment special was that the tutor brought in a visiting speaker who was a forensics expert and we got to do some of the things they have to do at the crime scene. We all had to wear full plastic bodysuits and masks so we didn't spoil the evidence and we had to search for clues and take photographs of the scene. We took photos of what we did and we were able to use them on our posters.

I really enjoy how practical the BTEC Level 2 First is and the variety of different assessments you can do. In my first year I have done posters, leaflets, presentations and demonstrations, and next year my tutor has talked about us making our own documentary. The practical assessments and the independence I have when doing them really suits me and I've been getting much better grades on my BTEC First work than my predicted GCSE grades.

Another assignment we did was in uniformed public service fitness – we had to take part in a public service fitness test. My fitness isn't really good and I was a bit shocked at how much I'm going to have to improve before I apply to a service in a couple of years, but it has made me join a gym and I'm trying to eat healthily. That's the thing about the assignments – it's not just another piece of work, they can actually affect how you live your life too!'

TOP TIPS

Doing your best in assignments involves several skills, including managing your time so that you don't get behind. See pages 25–28 for tips on managing your time more efficiently.

BTEC FACTS

On a BTEC course you achieve individual criteria at pass, merit or distinction for your assignments. You will receive a pass, merit or distinction **grade** for completed units and then one of these three grades for the whole course.

Getting the most from your BTEC

Getting the most from your BTEC involves several skills, such as using your time effectively and working well with other people. Knowing yourself is also important.

Knowing yourself

How would you describe yourself? Make some notes here.

If you described yourself to someone else, would you be able to sum up your temperament and personality, identify your strengths and weaknesses and list your skills? If not, is it because you've never thought about it or because you honestly don't have a clue?

Learning about yourself is often called self-analysis. You may have already done personality tests or careers profiles. If not, there are many available online. However, the information you gain from these profiles is useless unless you can apply it to what you are doing.

Your personality

Everyone is different. For example, some people:

- like to plan in advance; others prefer to be spontaneous
- love being part of a group; others prefer one or two close friends
- enjoy being the life and soul of the party; others prefer to sit quietly and feel uncomfortable at large social gatherings
- are imaginative and creative; others prefer to deal only with facts
- think carefully about all their options before making a decision; others follow their 'gut instincts' and often let their heart rule their head.

Case study: Your personality

It is really important to know about yourself and your personality before you consider joining the public services. The services aren't about who talks the loudest or who dominates the group. The public service sector in the UK has over 6 million employees so it's safe to say that all personality types can find a suitable job within this area.

Chen and Molly are both are studying for a BTEC Level 2 in Public Services, but they have very different personalities.

Chen is a very quiet young man who excels in written work, gaining distinctions in all his work. He is calm and organised and is always at his lessons on time and properly prepared. Chen is less able on the practical aspects of the course and in particular finds it difficult to speak out in group discussions or take a leadership role in practical activities.

Molly is very assertive and always willing to put her point across in group activities. She really enjoys the practical parts of the course and loves the fitness and residential activities her group has done so far. Molly is weaker on written work: she often leaves it until the last minute and doesn't hand it in on time.

Chen and Molly are very different, but the public services require both Chen's skills such as excellence in written work and a methodical approach to problem solving and Molly's skills such as assertiveness and teamwork. Both sets of skills can be equally useful, but on your BTEC Level 2 First course it makes sense to try and develop the areas you are weaker in so that you are a more balanced potential recruit.

Think about what you think your strengths and weaknesses are, and if you have any of the same development needs as Molly and Chen.

TRY THIS →

Imagine one of your friends is describing your best features. What would they say?

Personalities in the workplace

There's a mix of personalities in most workplaces. Some people prefer to work behind the scenes, such as many IT practitioners, who like to concentrate on tasks they enjoy doing. Others love high-profile jobs, where they may often be involved in high-pressure situations, such as paramedics and television presenters. Most people fall somewhere between these two extremes.

In any job there will be some aspects that are more appealing and interesting than others. If you have a part-time job you will already know this. The same thing applies to any course you take!

Your personality and your BTEC First course

Understanding your personality means you can identify which parts of your course you are likely to find easy and which more difficult. Working out the aspects you need to develop should be positive. You can also think about how your strengths and weaknesses may affect other people.

- Natural planners find it easier to schedule work for assignments.
- Extroverts like giving presentations and working with others but may overwhelm quieter team members.
- Introverts often prefer to work alone and may be excellent at researching information.

Activity: What is your personality type?

1a) Identify your own personality type, either by referring to a personality test you have done recently or by going online and doing a reliable test. Go to page 96 to find out how to access a useful website for this activity.

Print a summary of the completed test or write a brief description of the results for future reference.

b) Use this information to identify the tasks and personal characteristics that you find easy or difficult.

	Easy	Difficult
Being punctual		
Planning how to do a job		
Working neatly and accurately		
Being well organised		
Having good ideas		
Taking on new challenges		
Being observant		
Working with details		
Being patient		
Coping with criticism		
Dealing with customers		
Making decisions		
Keeping calm under stress		
Using your own initiative		

	Easy	Difficult
Researching facts carefully and accurately		
Solving problems		
Meeting deadlines		
Finding and correcting own errors		
Clearing up after yourself		
Helping other people		
Working as a member of a team		
Being sensitive to the needs of others		
Respecting other people's opinions		
Being tactful and discreet		
Being even-tempered		

2 Which thing from your 'difficult' list do you think you should work on improving first? Start by identifying the benefits you will gain. Then decide how to achieve your goal.

BTEC FACT

All BTEC First courses enable you to develop your personal, learning and thinking skills (**PLTS**), which will help you to meet new challenges more easily. (See page 87.)

Your knowledge and skills

You already have a great deal of knowledge, as well as practical and personal skills gained at school, at home and at work (if you have a part-time job). Now you need to assess these to identify your strengths and weaknesses.

To do this accurately, try to identify evidence for your knowledge and skills. Obvious examples are:

○ previous qualifications

○ school reports

○ occasions when you have demonstrated particular skills, such as communicating with customers or colleagues in a part-time job.

Part-time jobs give you knowledge and skills in a real work setting.

Activity: Check your skills

1 Score yourself from 1 to 5 for each of the skills in the table below.

   1 = I'm very good at this skill.

   2 = I'm good but could improve this skill.

   3 = This skill is only average and I know that I need to improve it.

   4 = I'm weak at this skill and must work hard to improve it.

   5 = I've never had the chance to develop this skill.

   Enter the score in the column headed 'Score A' and add today's date.

2 Look back at the units and topics you will be studying for your course – you entered them into the chart on page 9. Use this to identify any additional skills that you know are important for your course and add them to the table. Then score yourself for these skills, too.

3 Identify the main skills you will need in order to be successful in your chosen career, and highlight them in the table.

   Go back and score yourself against each skill after three, six and nine months. That way you can monitor your progress and check where you need to take action to develop the most important skills you will need.

English and communication skills	Score A (today) Date:	Score B (after three months) Date:	Score C (after six months) Date:	Score D (after nine months) Date:
Reading and understanding different types of texts and information				
Speaking to other people face to face				
Speaking clearly on the telephone				
Listening carefully				
Writing clearly and concisely				
Presenting information in a logical order				
Summarising information				
Using correct punctuation and spelling				
Joining in a group discussion				
Expressing your own ideas and opinions appropriately				
Persuading other people to do something				
Making an oral presentation and presenting ideas clearly				
ICT skills	Score A (today) Date:	Score B (after three months) Date:	Score C (after six months) Date:	Score D (after nine months) Date:
Using ICT equipment correctly and safely				
Using a range of software				
Accurate keyboarding				
Proofreading				
Using the Internet to find and select appropriate information				
Using ICT equipment to communicate and exchange information				
Producing professional documents which include tables and graphics				
Creating and interpreting spreadsheets				
Using PowerPoint				

Maths and numeracy skills	Score A (today) Date:	Score B (after three months) Date:	Score C (after six months) Date:	Score D (after nine months) Date:
Carrying out calculations (eg money, time, measurements, etc.) in a work-related situation				
Estimating amounts				
Understanding and interpreting data in tables, graphs, diagrams and charts				
Comparing prices and identifying best value for money				
Solving routine and non-routine work-related numerical problems				

Case study: Your knowledge and skills

People decide to do a BTEC Level 2 First in Public Services for many different reasons. Some have family members in the services or have a background in the army or police cadets, which has helped them decide what job they want to do. Others have seen public service-based televisions shows such as *CSI* or *The Bill* and have used that as a basis for deciding what they would like to do.

Kalum's family have a long history in the services as both of his parents were in the army. His mum now works as a police officer and his dad works for the council and is a part-time retained firefighter. They encouraged Kalum's interest in the services from a very young age and he joined the police cadets as soon as he was old enough.

Charli has never been in the cadets and none of her family

have a background in the services, but she has always really enjoyed science and, after going on a forensics visit with school, she decided that she wanted to be a scene of crime officer in the Police Service.

Kalum and Charli both bring different skills and abilities to the course. Kalum has experienced the discipline and types of work done by the services and has the experience of his parents' careers to draw upon and the support of his family in his job choice.

Charli brings to her course a keen interest in the scientific aspects of the services and lots of background knowledge on how the services might use forensics to help solve problems.

Think about how your interest in the services began.

Managing your time

Some people are brilliant at managing their time. They do everything they need to and have time left over for activities they enjoy. Other people complain that they don't know where the time goes.

Which are you? If you need help to manage your time – and most people do – you will find help here.

Why time management is important

- It means you stay in control, get less stressed and don't skip important tasks.
- Some weeks will be peaceful, others will be hectic.
- The amount of homework and assignments you have to do will vary.
- As deadlines approach, time always seems to go faster.
- Some work will need to be done quickly, maybe for the next lesson; other tasks may need to be done over several days or weeks. This needs careful planning.
- You may have several assignments or tasks to complete in a short space of time.
- You want to have a social life.

Avoiding time–wasting

We can all plan to do work, and then find our plans go wrong. There may be several reasons for this. How many of the following do *you* do?

	Top time-wasting activities
1	Allowing (or encouraging) people to interrupt you.
2	Not having the information, handouts or textbook you need because you've lost them or lent them to someone else.
3	Chatting to people, making calls or sending texts when you should be working.
4	Getting distracted because you simply must keep checking out MySpace, Facebook or emails.
5	Putting off jobs until they are a total nightmare, then panicking.
6	Daydreaming.
7	Making a mess of something so you have to start all over again.

TOP TIPS

Learning to prioritise means that you do what's important and urgent *first*. This means checking deadlines carefully. A task may be urgent and important if not doing it might delay you later – such as sending off for information that could take a while to arrive.

Planning and getting organised

The first step in managing your time is to plan ahead and be well organised. Some people are naturally good at this. They think ahead, write down their commitments in a diary or planner, and store their notes and handouts neatly and carefully so they can find them quickly.

How good are your working habits?

Talking to friends can take up a lot of time.

Improving your planning and organisational skills

1 Use a diary or planner to schedule working times into your weekdays and weekends.

2 Have a place for everything and everything in its place.

3 Be strict with yourself when you start work. If you aren't really in the mood, set a shorter time limit and give yourself a reward when the time is up.

4 Keep a diary in which you write down exactly what work you have to do.

5 Divide up long or complex tasks into manageable chunks and put each 'chunk' in your diary with a deadline of its own.

6 Write a 'to do' list if you have several different tasks. Tick them off as you go.

7 Always allow more time than you think you need for a task.

TRY THIS

Analyse your average day.

How many hours do you spend sleeping, eating, travelling, attending school or college, working and taking part in leisure activities?

How much time is left for homework and assignments?

Case study: Avoiding time-wasters

Ben considers his social life.

'I've always liked going out – when I was younger I was always out on my bike or with friends and now I'm either out with my mates or my girlfriend. I don't like to be stuck in the house so I'll pretty much go out at the drop of a hat even if I haven't got anywhere in particular to go.

When I first started the BTEC Level 2 First in Public Services the tutor told us that because of the coursework required we would have to set aside some home study time to make sure we kept up with the work. I was planning to do this and even sorted out my desk and nagged my mum for a new computer. The problem was I'd sit down with the intention of doing the work and then the phone would ring and my mates would be out or my girlfriend wanted to come round and I'd drop the work and do whatever else was on offer.

The result was I started missing pretty much all my deadlines and the tutor said I was at risk of failing the course. I was gutted with myself and I had a talk with my mum and we agreed a plan to help me pass. The first thing was that when I came in she would take my mobile off me until my work was finished. That way I couldn't get distracted by my mates calling and wanting to go out. I also had a word with my girlfriend and we have set aside specific times to see each other, that way neither of us risks getting behind with our work. I'm really disappointed that I didn't have the self-discipline to stop getting into this position but really pleased I've managed to get myself back on track.'

Does Ben's situation sound familiar? Do you spend a lot of time in chatrooms? Do you put your social life before your studies?

TOP TIPS

If you become distracted by social networking sites or email when you're working, set yourself a time limit of 10 minutes or so to indulge yourself.

BTEC FACT

If you have serious problems that are interfering with your ability to work or to concentrate, talk to your tutor. There are many ways in which BTEC learners who have personal difficulties can be supported to help them continue with their studies.

Activity: Managing time

1 The correct term for something you do in preference to starting a particular task is a 'displacement activity'. In the workplace this includes things like often going to the water cooler to get a drink, and constantly checking emails and so on online. People who work from home may tidy up, watch television or even cook a meal to put off starting a job.

Write down *your* top three displacement activities.

2 Today is Wednesday. Sajid has several jobs to do tonight and has started well by making a 'to do' list. He's worried that he won't get through all the things on his list and because he works on Thursday and Friday evenings that the rest will have to wait until Saturday.

a) Look through Sajid's list and decide which jobs are top priority and *must* be done tonight and which can be left until Saturday if he runs out of time.

b) Sajid is finding that his job is starting to interfere with his ability to do his assignments. What solutions can you suggest to help him?

Jobs to do

- File handouts from today's classes

- Phone Tom (left early today) to tell him the time of our presentation tomorrow has been changed to 11 am

- Research information online for next Tuesday's lesson

- Complete table from rough notes in class today

- Rewrite section of leaflet to talk about at tutorial tomorrow

- Write out class's ideas for the charity of the year, ready for course representatives meeting tomorrow lunchtime

- Redo handout Tom and I are giving out at presentation

- Plan how best to schedule assignment received today – deadline 3 weeks

- Download booklet from website ready for next Monday's class

TRY THIS ➡

Write down your current commitments and how long they take each week. Then decide those that are top priority and those that you could postpone in a very busy week.

Getting the most from work experience

On some BTEC First courses, all learners have to do a **work placement**. On others, they are recommended but not essential, or are required only for some optional units. If you are doing one, you need to prepare for it so that you get the most out of it. The checklists in this section will help.

Before you go checklist

1 Find out about the organisation by researching online.

2 Check that you have all the information you'll need about the placement.

3 Check the route you will need to take and how long it will take you. Always allow longer on the first day.

4 Check with your tutor what clothes are suitable and make sure you look the part.

5 Check that you know any rules or guidelines you must follow.

6 Check that you know what to do if you have a serious problem during the placement, such as being too ill to go to work.

7 Talk to your tutor if you have any special personal concerns.

8 Read the unit(s) that relate to your placement carefully. Highlight points you need to remember or refer to regularly.

9 Read the assessment criteria that relate to the unit(s) and use these to make a list of the information and evidence you'll need to obtain.

10 Your tutor will give you an official log book or diary – or just use a notebook. Make notes each evening while things are fresh in your mind, and keep them safely.

While you're on work placement

Ideally, on your first day you'll be told about the business and what you'll be expected to do. You may even be allocated to one particular member of staff who will be your 'mentor'. However, not all firms operate like this and if everyone is very busy, your **induction** may be rushed. If so, stay positive and watch other people to see what they're doing. Then offer to help where you can.

BTEC FACT

If you need specific evidence from a work placement for a particular unit, your tutor may give you a log book or work diary, and will tell you how you will be assessed in relation to the work that you will do.

TRY THIS

You're on work experience. The placement is interesting and related to the job you want to do. However, you've been watching people most of the time and want to get more involved. Identify three jobs you think you could offer to do.

While you're there

1. Arrive with a positive attitude, knowing that you are going to do your best and get the most out of your time there.

2. Although you may be nervous at first, don't let that stop you from smiling at people, saying 'hello' and telling them your name.

3. Arrive punctually – or even early – every day. If you're delayed for any reason, phone and explain. Then get there as soon as you can.

4. If you take your mobile phone, switch it off when you arrive.

5. If you have nothing to do, offer to help someone who is busy or ask if you can watch someone who is doing a job that interests you.

6. Always remember to thank people who give you information, show you something or agree that you can observe them.

7. If you're asked to do something and don't understand what to do, ask for it to be repeated. If it's complicated, write it down.

8. If a task is difficult, start it and then check back that you are doing it correctly before you go any further.

9. Obey all company rules, such as regulations and procedures relating to health and safety and using machinery, the use of IT equipment and access to confidential information.

10. Don't rush off as fast as you can at the end of the day. Check first with your mentor or supervisor whether you can leave.

Coping with problems

Problems are rare but can happen. The most common ones are being bored because you're not given any work to do or upset because you feel someone is treating you unfairly. Normally, the best first step is to talk to your mentor at work or your supervisor. However, if you're very worried or upset, you may prefer to get in touch with your tutor instead – do it promptly.

TOP TIPS

Observing people who are skilled at what they do helps you learn a lot, and may even be part of your **assignment brief.**

Getting experience of work in the public services sector

Getting work placements anywhere can be a challenge, but it can be very difficult to get a placement in a public service. This is because the armed and emergency services do operational work for most of their working day: they are doing the actual job of putting out fires, arresting people, recovering casualties or are deployed in conflict situations. This means that you could be in danger if they took you along and because you are untrained in the job you may put other people's lives at risk. It may be easier to find a placement in a non-uniformed public service such as your local council, your local community centre or a local school or college. The non-uniformed services value the contribution that work placement brings and you will benefit from working in a team in a safe and supportive environment.

However it is possible to arrange placements in any public service if you are sensible about what you can and can't do. For longer term work experience all three armed services have cadet units in most areas, as do the police, and some fire and rescue services have young firefighter initiatives.

One of the better ways of getting work experience in the services is to approach your local council or charities as they are both heavily involved in the public service sector. Youth clubs and charities such as Victim Support and St John Ambulance can give you an insight into what working for the public services really is all about.

So how would you find a placement?

It really depends on which service you want a placement with. Details of cadet groups for the armed and emergency services or contacts at the local council or charities can usually be found by doing a quick Internet search or calling the service in person. The numbers can be found online or in your local phone book. Your tutor may also be able to help by contacting companies on your behalf and allowing you time away from your studies to do a short placement.

Looking at cadet detachments

Most cadet groups meet once or twice a week in the evening and may be based on school premises, police stations or Territorial Army bases. Are you prepared to travel to these under your own steam? Can you give up one or two evenings a week to train and possibly some weekends for additional work? Can you accept the discipline that goes along with cadet work? Would the work you do with the cadets be useful for your BTEC First? Many army cadets already do the BTEC Level 2 First in Public Services as part of their training. Would this clash with your school or college programme or make you better prepared?

Deciding to volunteer with the non-uniformed public services

Your local council is an excellent start if you are planning to secure a work placement in a non-uniformed public service. They run all of the public facilities in your area such as libraries, leisure centres and community centres and they also have a large range of departments, which deal with services from housing to environmental health to social work. This provides you with plenty of possible options for a work placement experience and most local councils are happy to take you on for a week or two at a time.

Deciding to volunteer for a charity

It is likely that you will be required to work set hours either during the day or at weekends. How does this fit in with your studies and your personal life? Do you believe in what the charity is doing? Do you support their aims? If not, working for them might not help you as much as you think.

When you apply for a service the work you have done in the community will be very important to the people who interview you. It can form a key part of the recruiting process. Consider the following conversation:

Police Recruiting Officer: So tell me, why do you want to be a police officer?

Kyle: I've wanted to be a police officer since I was little. It looks like a great job being able to help people all the time – helping people is really rewarding.

Police Recruiting Officer: So you like helping the community?

Kyle: Definitely, helping the community and the people in it is a key part of being a police officer and it's very important to me.

Police Recruiting Officer: So if helping the community is so important why haven't you actually done any community work?

Kyle: Ummm...

The services value the experience of people who give up their own time to serve the community whether in cadets or another way. It shows a genuine commitment and means you have thought about your career seriously.

Activity: Advantages and disadvantages of placements

What are the advantages and disadvantages of public service work placements or cadet involvement? Complete the table below. Examples have been given in both columns to start you off.

Advantages	Disadvantages
Learning more about the particular job you want to do to see if it's right for you.	Takes time away from your studies or your social life.

Do you think cadet or volunteering is the way forward for you? If not what can you do to help a recruiting officer take you seriously?

Case study: Army residential course

Yasmin was lucky enough to be selected for a five-day Army residential 'look at life' course. The course is designed to give young people a taste of army life and the skills and abilities that are needed to be a success in the armed services. The course was organised by Yasmin's centre and she was accompanied by three tutors and 29 other BTEC First in Public Services students.

Yasmin was very keen to be in the army and particularly wanted to join the Royal Signals Regiment, but she was not prepared for the reality of army life. The course began at 6.30 in the morning with fitness training and didn't stop until 11 p.m. after night navigation exercises. The work, although lots of fun and very interesting, was physically demanding and emotionally exhausting. The course has caused Yasmin to rethink what she wants to do in her career. At home Yasmin is the youngest child and her brothers and sisters have all either left home or gone to university. She knows she has been babied by her parents since she is the youngest and she wonders if this has influenced how difficult she found the week.

Working with other people

Everyone finds it easy to work with people they like and far harder with those they don't. On your course you'll often be expected to work as a team to do a task. This gives you practice in working with different people.

You will be expected to:

- contribute to the task
- listen to other people's views
- adapt to other people's ways of working
- take responsibility for your own contribution
- agree the best way to resolve any problems.

These are quite complex skills. It helps if you understand the benefits to be gained by working cooperatively with other people and know the best way to achieve this.

BTEC FACT

An important part of your BTEC course is learning how to work positively and productively with other people.

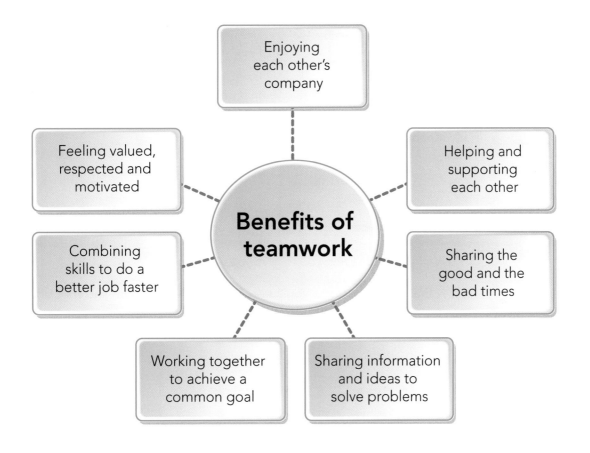

The benefits of good working relationships and teamwork.

Golden rules for everyone (including the team leader!)

The secret of a successful team is that everyone works together. The role of the team leader is to make this as easy as possible by listening to people's views and coordinating everyone's efforts. A team leader is not there to give orders.

Positive teamwork checklist

✔ Be loyal to your team, including the team leader.

✔ Be reliable and dependable at all times.

✔ Be polite. Remember to say 'please' and 'thank you'.

✔ Think before you speak.

✔ Treat everyone the same.

✔ Make allowances for individual personalities. Give people 'space' if they need it, but be ready to offer support if they ask for it.

✔ Admit mistakes and apologise if you've done something wrong – learn from it but don't dwell on it.

✔ Give praise when it's due, give help when you can and thank people who help you.

✔ Keep confidences, and any promises that you make.

Do you:

a) shrug and say nothing in case he gets upset

b) ask why he didn't text you to give you warning

c) say that it's the last time you'll ever go anywhere with him and walk off?

Which do you think would be the most effective – and why?

Case study: Teamwork in public services

Working as part of a team is an essential part of public service work. It is unusual for members of the public services to work alone; teams, pairs and small groups are much more usual. Different types of team can be found across the different public services, from crews, regiments and multi-agency teams, to project teams working on implementing new policies and specialist teams such as search and rescue.

One of the units you may complete on your BTEC Level 2 First in Public Services is Unit 15: Expedition Skills in Public Services. This unit requires you to work in teams to complete a multi-day expedition, which is obviously going to require significant amounts of teamwork and cooperation.

Students at a college in the Dearne Valley are about to begin planning their expedition. They need to ensure everyone has clear roles and responsibilities to make sure they take all the appropriate equipment and are able to complete their expedition in safety. Their tutor asks them to decide how they are going to approach the planning and they decide to do the following:

1 Set up a short list of ground rules about how they are going to work with each other. The list includes listening to each other's points of view, always doing what they have agreed to do and not letting down other team members.

2 Set up a list of aims and objectives about the expedition, including what kind of route to take, how far to walk and where to camp.

3 Organise a schedule of regular meetings so they are always in touch and can deal with any problems that arise in the planning process.

4 Set roles and responsibilities for each team member, which are then placed in an action plan for each team member to sign and for the tutor to have a copy of as part of their evidence for the unit.

Now think about if there is anything else you would add to this list.

There are many benefits to be gained from working as a team.

Activity: Teamwork in classroom tasks

The BTEC Level 2 First in Public Services is a course that has lots of opportunities built in for teamwork. One of the most common things you are likely to come across is paired or small group assessment activities where you work with others to produce a piece of work for your tutor to mark.

This has the advantage of being able to use other people's expertise to improve your work but can have real drawbacks if the team doesn't work well together or some team members don't pull their weight.

When working in groups to produce assessed work what can you do to ensure your group works well together and produces good quality work? Think of at least three things and list them below.

You will often find that you are in groups with very different people who you may not know well or even may not like. In the services you must be able to work with a variety of team members without letting your personal views affect how you work.

Describe three things you could do that would help you work effectively with people you don't know very well. List them below.

One of the disadvantages of group work is that your overall grade is dependent upon the work of others rather than just your own efforts. This also means that other people's grades are dependent on you. This is a big responsibility and it means you may have to work that bit harder to ensure you don't let your team members down – they will be relying on you. Some of the things your team can do to help get the best possible grades in group work are:

- Spend time together in the library doing joint research. After all, two heads are better than one.
- Draw up an action plan so that everyone knows which aspects of the work they are responsible for.
- Get together before the work is due in to make sure everyone has done their share.
- Make sure you all have a full copy of the work so that if one of your team is ill or absent you can still meet your deadlines.

There will be occasions when you are working with a team that doesn't seem to work very well together. This is a real problem as all of your grades may suffer.

Describe three things you can do to help the team get back on track and produce work of a high standard.

1
2
3

Activity: Teamwork in practical tasks

As well as offering the opportunity to work in teams for classroom assessments, the BTEC First in Public Services also has lots of opportunities for working together on practical tasks such as role plays, simulations, fitness programmes, initiative tests, assault courses and residential activities.

This means that being able to work together in a practical environment is as important as being able to work together in a classroom or library. Practical tasks require you to know more about the strengths and weaknesses of your team so that each person can be matched to the best task for them. For example, if someone is very good at map and compass work it makes sense for them to take the lead when navigating and assisting others to develop those skills. If one team member is well practised in radio communication protocols it make sense for them to take the lead on that and help the rest of the group improve.

The trick is finding out what your team are good at. One way of doing this is to use a SWOT analysis. SWOT stands for Strengths, Weaknesses, Opportunities and Threats. You could use a simplified version to help you discover what your team members are good at and where they may need help.

Consider the last time you were part of a team and complete the tables based on the strengths and weaknesses of each team member.

Team Member: _____

Strengths	Weaknesses

Team Member: _____

Strengths	Weaknesses

Team Member: _____

Strengths	Weaknesses

Doing this activity before you start your teamwork may help to avoid problems and point to where the stronger members of the team could help the weaker members to develop their skills.

Another key aspect of practical tasks is good communication – your team must know what they are doing and why if they are to achieve it successfully. Nothing can harm teamwork more than poor communication and a lack of respect for each other's opinions and ideas.

For example, a small group of BTEC First in Public Services students have been asked to prepare a role play of a road traffic incident that all of the emergency services will attend. This is the type of activity that might be set by your tutor in units such as Unit 1: Public Service Skills and Unit 17: Working in Incident Services.

Lots of different ideas are put forward about the role play and what the scenario could be. One student is a police cadet and has repeatedly made negative comments about the ideas of the rest of the team. She thinks she knows more about how the services work because she is a cadet. Her comments have included things such as:

- The police would never do it that way. You don't know what you are talking about.

- I'm a cadet and I know more than you do. You should shut up and listen to me.

What would be the effects of these comments on:

1 The student she is talking to?

2 The rest of the group?

3 Her own reputation in the group – how would the rest of the learners feel about her?

Many of the public services operate a strict rank structure where leaders make the decisions and the rest of the team members follow them, but good leaders will usually ask for ideas and contributions from their team – it would be a waste of the team's talents if they did not. If you are a leader in your team ensure you listen to each team member's ideas with respect even if you do not agree with them.

Getting the most from special events

BTEC First courses usually include several practical activities and special events. These enable you to find out information, develop your skills and knowledge in new situations and enjoy new experiences. They may include visits to external venues, visits from specialist speakers, and team events.

This police officer is telling a group of BTEC First learners about life in the police force and the specialist skills he needs to do his job.

Most learners enjoy the chance to do something different. You'll probably look forward to some events more than others. If you're ready to get actively involved, you'll usually gain the most benefit. It also helps to make a few preparations!

Case study: Navy residential trip

Sally had the opportunity to go on a four-day residential to Faslane Naval Base in Scotland as part of her work on the First Diploma at Summerhill Academy.

'I was really excited to go on the trip to Scotland because the lads on my course had a great time visiting the Marines and I thought it was only fair we should have a chance to go with the Navy too. My best friend Becka was on the trip too so I knew we would have a good time.

We did some amazing things, such as dry slope skiing, paintballing and lots of sports, but there were a couple of things that really stood out for me, one of which was the battle swimming test. We had to swim 50 metres in these really baggy overalls and tread water for two minutes. Then we had to get out of the pool by ourselves with no help. I was really tired but really pleased I'd passed.

We also went aboard a mine hunter ship, had a tour and spoke to naval ratings. The things they told us were really interesting and you couldn't find them out in books. One rating told us that on this particular design of mine hunter ship the sleeping accommodation was at one end rather than in the middle, which made seasickness a really bad problem in rough weather.

The absolute best thing of all was that a Vanguard class nuclear submarine was at the base for repairs and we were allowed on it for a tour. Women aren't allowed to serve as submariners so it was a rare treat to be allowed on board. I couldn't believe how small everything is – nine guys have to sleep in triple-decker bunk beds in a room about half the size of my bedroom.

The whole trip was amazing. I definitely want to join the Navy now and I think lots of my friends are considering it too. The trip really helped me with some of my BTEC work too as I have seen and done in person some of the things we talk about in class. Another benefit is that my friends who want to join a non-uniformed service really enjoyed the experience as well as it gave them the opportunity to improve their teamwork, cooperation, leadership and communication skills, which are needed in all the public services.'

TRY THIS

At the last minute, you're asked to propose a vote of thanks to a visiting speaker on behalf of your class. What would you say?

Special events checklist

- ✔ Check you understand how the event relates to your course.

- ✔ If a visit or trip is not something you would normally find very interesting, try to keep an open mind. You might get a surprise!

- ✔ Find out what you're expected to do, and any rules or guidelines you must follow, including about your clothes or appearance.

- ✔ Always allow enough time to arrive five minutes early, and make sure you're never late.

- ✔ On an external visit, make notes on what you see and hear. This is essential if you have to write about it afterwards, use your information to answer questions in an assignment or do something practical.

- ✔ If an external speaker is going to talk to your class, prepare a list of questions in advance. Nominate someone to thank the speaker afterwards. If you want to record the talk, it's polite to ask first.

- ✔ For a team event, you may be involved in planning and helping to allocate different team roles. You'll be expected to participate positively in any discussions, to talk for some (but not all) of the time, and perhaps to volunteer for some jobs yourself.

- ✔ Write up any notes you make as soon as you can – while you can still understand what you wrote!

Activity: Visiting public service personnel

Your BTEC Level 2 First in Public Services course may have some input from visiting public service personnel. These visitors are usually currently working in a public service and will be giving up their own time to come into school or college to tell you about service life and answer your questions, or you may go out to their place of work and speak with them there. They are also really useful sources of information, which may help you when completing your assessed work.

Preparing for a visit to public service premises or meeting with public service personnel

Before your visitor arrives or you visit their place of work it is a good idea to do some research on the type of organisation they represent and the type of work they do.

Consider the following:

1 Which service are they from?
2 What type of work do they do in that service?
3 Are they a civilian?
4 How long have they been in the service?
5 How does that service link with other public services?
6 How will the information given by the public service personnel help with your assignments?

There are some general rules of behaviour when you go on a visit to a public service place of work or you meet with public service personnel.

1 Be polite and respectful at all times.

2 Think about the role of the person and the organisation and consider the questions you might want to ask them about the organisation and their role within it.

3 Make a good impression with your body language.

4 Take notes.

5 Show interest in the topic.

6 Turn off your mobile phone.

Remember that the person speaking to you may be involved in the recruitment process for that organisation so it's important to try and make a good impression.

Use the following grid to help you make notes when you visit public service premises or meet with a member of the public services.

Name:	
Public Service organisation:	
Job/Rank:	
Topic covered	Information
Topic 1 _____	
Topic 2 _____	
Topic 3 _____	
Which assignment is this information most useful for?	
Where can I go to find more information?	
What questions do I need to ask of the speaker at the end of their talk?	

Resources and research

Understanding resources

Resources are items that help you do something. The most obvious one is money! To obtain your BTEC First award, however, your resources are rather different.

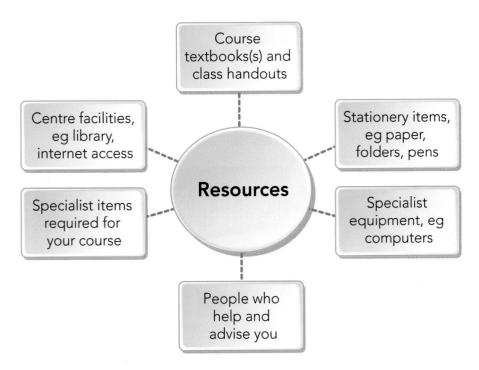

Different kinds of resources

Physical resources

Physical resources are things like textbooks, computers and any specialist equipment.

- Popular textbooks, laptops for home use and specialist equipment may need to be booked. Leaving it until the last minute is risky.
- You can ask for help if you don't know how to use resources properly.
- You should check what stationery and equipment you need at the start of your course and make sure you have it.
- You need to look after your resources carefully. This saves money and time spent replacing lost items.

People as resources

There are many people who can help you through your course:
- family members who help and support you
- your tutor
- friends in your group who collect handouts for you and phone you to keep you up-to-date when you're absent
- librarians and computer technicians, at your centre or your local library
- expert practitioners.

Expert practitioners

Expert practitioners have worked hard to be successful in their chosen area. They know the skills and knowledge needed to do the job properly. They can be invaluable when you're researching information. You can also learn a lot by watching them at work, especially if you can ask them questions about what they do, what they find hard and any difficulties they've had.

Expert practitioners must possess certain skills in order to be successful in their chosen field. For example, this firefighter must know how to think on his feet in an emergency situation.

Try to observe more than one expert practitioner:
- It gives you a better picture about what they do.
- No single job will cover all aspects of work that might apply to your studies.
- You may find some experts more approachable and easy to understand than others. For example, if someone is impatient because they're busy it may be difficult to ask them questions, or if someone works very quickly you may find it hard to follow what they're doing.

If you have problems, just note what you've learned and compare it with your other observations. And there's always the chance that you're observing someone who's not very good at their job! You'll only know this for certain if you've seen what people should be doing.

Activity: Creating a resource list

There is no shortage of resources for public service students as there are lots of books and journals around that cover all aspects of the services. In addition, every service has a comprehensive website with all the information you could possibly want or need about the work they do.

Use the grid below to make a list of the resources you think you may need on your BTEC Level 2 First Diploma.

Resource	What do I need?
Books	
Journals	
Internet	
Newspapers	
Stationery	
Specialist equipment	
Other resources	

Finding the information you need

The information explosion

There are lots of different ways to find out information – books, newspapers, magazines, TV, radio, CDs, DVDs, the internet. And you can exchange information with other people by texting, sending an email or phoning someone.

All this makes it much easier to obtain information. If you know what you're doing, you can probably find most of what you need sitting at a computer. But there are some dangers:

- Finding exactly what you want online takes skill. You need to know what you're doing.
- It's easy to get too much information and become overwhelmed.
- It's unlikely that everything you need will be available online.
- The information you read may be out of date.
- The information may be neither reliable nor true.

Define what you are trying to find. (The more precise you are, the more likely you are to find what you're looking for.)

Know where to look for it. (Remember: the internet is not the only source of information.)

Recognise when you have found appropriate information.

Know what to do with information once you've found it. (Make sure that you understand it, interpret it correctly and record the source where you found it.)

Know when to stop looking (especially if you have a deadline).

Finding and using information effectively

Before you start

There are four things that will help you look in the right place and target your search properly.

Ask yourself ...	Because ...	Example
Exactly what do I need to find out?	It will save you time and effort.	If you need information about accidents, you need to know what type of accident and over what time period.
Why do I need this information and who is going to read it?	This puts the task into context. You need to identify the best type of information to obtain and how to get it.	If you're making a poster or leaflet for children, you'll need simple information that can be presented in a graphical format. If, however, you're giving a workplace presentation on accidents, you'll need tables and graphs to illustrate your talk.
Where can I find it?	You need to consider whether your source is trustworthy and up to date. The internet is great, but you must check that the sites you use are reliable.	To find out about accidents in the workplace you could talk to the health and safety at work officer. To find examples of accidents in your local area you could look through back copies of your local newspaper in the local library or newspaper offices.
What is my deadline?	You know how long you have to find the information and use it.	

Your three main sources of information are:
- libraries or learning resource centres
- the internet
- other people, for example asking questions through interviews and questionnaires.

Researching in libraries

You can use the learning resource centre in your school or college, or a local public library. Public libraries usually have a large reference section with many resources available for loan, including CD-ROMs, encyclopaedias, government statistics, magazines, journals and newspapers, and databases such as Infotrac, which contains articles from newspapers and magazines over the last five years.

The librarian will show you how to find the resources you need and how to look up a specific book (or author) to check if it is available or is out on loan.

TRY THIS

Schedule your research time by calculating backwards from the deadline date. Split the time you have 50/50 between searching for information and using it. This stops you searching for too long and getting lots of interesting material, but then not having the time to use it properly!

Some books and resources can only be used in the library itself, while others can be taken out on short-term or long-term loan. You need to plan how to access and use the resources that are popular or restricted.

Using your library

✔ If your centre has an intranet you might be able to check which books and CD-ROMs are available without actually visiting the library.

✔ All libraries have photocopying facilities, so take enough change with you to copy articles that you can't remove. Write down the source of any article you photocopy, ie the name and the date of the publication.

✔ Learn how to keep a reference file (or bibliography) in which you store the details of all your sources and references. A bibliography must include CDs, DVDs and other information formats, not just books and magazines.

✔ If your search is complicated, go at a quiet time when the librarian can help you.

✔ Don't get carried away if you find several books that contain the information you need. Too many can be confusing.

✔ Use the index to find information quickly by searching for key words. Scan the index using several likely alternatives.

✔ Only use books that you find easy to understand. A book is only helpful if you can retell the information in your own words.

TRY THIS

Search engines don't just find websites. On Google, the options at the top of your screen include 'images', 'news' and 'maps'. If you click on 'more' and then 'even more', you'll find other options, too. You'll usually find the most relevant information if you use the UK version of a search engine. Only search the whole web if you deliberately want to include European and American information. Go to page 96 to find out how to see this in action.

Researching online

A good search engine such as Google will help you find useful websites. They look for sites based on the information you enter in the search box. In some cases, such as Ask.co.uk, you may get the chance to refine your choice after entering your key words or question.

Finding information on a website

Wikipedia is a popular free online encyclopaedia. It has been criticised because entries may be inaccurate as members of the public can edit the site. However, Wikipedia is trying to prevent this by organising professional editing.

If you're not sure whether something you read is correct, or if there is anything strange about it, check it against information on another site. Make sure you ask your tutor's opinion, too.

With large websites, it can be difficult to find what you need. Always read the whole screen – there may be several menus in different parts of the screen.

To help you search, many large websites have:
- their own search facility or a site map that lists site content with links to the different pages
- links to similar sites where you might find more information. Clicking a link should open a new window, so you'll still be connected to the original site.

There may be useful information and links at the top, foot or either side of a web page.

There are several other useful sites you could visit when researching online.

- **Directory sites** show websites in specific categories so you can focus your search at the start.

- **Forums** are sites, or areas of a website, where people post comments on an issue. They can be useful if you want to find out opinions on a topic. You can usually read them without registering.

- **News sites** include the BBC website as well as the sites for all the daily newspapers. Check the website of your local newspaper, too.

Printing information

- Only print information that you're sure will be useful. It's easy to print too much and find yourself drowning in paper.

- Make quick notes on your print-outs so that you remember why you wanted them. It will jog your memory when you're sorting through them later.

- If there's a printer-friendly option, use it. It will give you a print-out without unnecessary graphics or adverts.

- Check the bottom line of your print-outs. It should show the URL for that page of the website, and the date. You need those if you have to list your sources or if you want to quote from the page.

TRY THIS

Go to page 96 to find out how to see how directory sites work.

TOP TIPS

Bookmark sites you use regularly by adding the URL to your browser. How to do this will depend on which browser you use, eg Internet Explorer, Firefox.

Researching by asking other people

You're likely to do this for two reasons:

- you need help from someone who knows a lot about a topic
- you need to find out several people's opinions on something.

Information from an expert

Explain politely why you are carrying out the investigation. Ask questions slowly and clearly about what they do and how they do it. If they don't mind, you could take written notes so you remember what they tell you. Put the name and title of the person, and the date, at the top. This is especially important if you might be seeing more than one person, to avoid getting your notes muddled up.

Ask whether you may contact them again, in case there's anything you need to check. Write down their phone number or email address. Above all, remember to say 'thank you'!

The opinions of several people

The easiest way to do this is with a questionnaire. You can either give people the questionnaire to complete themselves or interview them and complete it yourself. Professional interviewers often telephone people to ask questions, but at this stage it's not a good idea unless you know the people you're phoning and they're happy for you to do this.

Devising a questionnaire

1. Make sure it has a title and clear instructions.

2. Rather than ask for opinions, give people options, eg yes/no, maybe/always, never/sometimes. This will make it easier to analyse the results.

3. Or you can ask interviewees to give a score, say out of 5, making it clear what each number represents, eg 5 = excellent, 3 = very good.

4. Keep your questionnaire short so that your interviewees don't lose interest. Between 10 and 15 questions is probably about right, as long as that's enough to find out all you need.

5. Remember to add 'thank you' at the end.

6. Decide upon the representative sample of people you will approach. These are the people whose views are the most relevant to the topic you're investigating.

7. Decide how many responses you need to get a valid answer. This means that the answer is representative of the wider population. For example, if you want views on food in your canteen, it's pointless only asking five people. You might pick the only five people who detest (or love) the food it serves.

TOP TIPS

Design your questionnaire so that you get quantifiable answers. This means you can easily add them up to get your final result.

TRY THIS

Always test your draft questionnaire on several people, to highlight any confusing questions or instructions.

Case study: Group research project

One of the most effective ways of finding out information in the public services is to ask someone. James and his team are completing a piece of work for an assessed task where they have to describe the roles and responsibilities of four different public services.

As the team leader, James has decided that it would be quicker and fairer if each member of the team conducts research into a different service and then brings their research to a team meeting, where the team will work together in creating the final presentation.

James makes an appointment with the Probation Service to gather his information on the roles and responsibilities of the service. He travels to the nearest office in the local town centre, has a chat with the officer and collects leaflets and booklets about the service.

Aaron's next door neighbour is a volunteer with Victim Support so this seems a sensible choice for him to investigate. Aaron goes round to his neighbour's for a discussion about the type of work he does. He then goes on to the Victim Support website for additional information.

Nafeesa's uncle is a firefighter so she asks him to help her find out about the roles and responsibilities of the Fire Service. Nafeesa is really lucky as her uncle arranges for a tour of his station and a chat with the station officer. She gathers plenty of information about what the Fire and Rescue Service does.

Barney researches the roles and responsibilities of HM Prison Service. He decides to focus on internet sites and uses the research he finds there to take back to the rest of the team.

Keeping a logbook

Some of the practical work you do on your BTEC First in Public Services may require you to keep a log of events as evidence. For example, your fitness unit requires you to plan and undertake a physical training programme and you will need to produce some form of ongoing evidence – a logbook is a sensible way of doing this.

Keeping a logbook can be difficult as it is easy to get distracted by other things and forget to fill it in. A good logbook should be filled in as soon as you have done the task so that your comments are fresh in your mind. It should also be neat and legible as it is likely your tutor will want to see the book as part of your assessment.

Below is an example of a fitness log completed by a student undertaking Unit 5: Improving Health and Fitness for Entry to the Uniformed Public Services.

Name: Alex Farmer	
Course: BTEC Level 2 First Diploma in Public Services	
Unit and criteria: Unit 5: Improving Health and Fitness for Entry to the Uniformed Public Services P6	

Which service test do you want to improve your performance on and why?

I need to improve my performance on the shuttle run and the press ups and sit up sessions of the police fitness test. We did all the tests today as part of our fitness assignment and they are the ones I failed.

Describe your training programme

I will be doing a mile run three times a week.

I will be going to the college gym twice a week to complete a fitness training programme designed for me by the gym instructor. It contains 20 mins of cardio on the cross trainer, bike and rower and then sets of repetitions on the weights.

I will be practising my sit ups and press ups per minute twice a week.

I will give up smoking and try to eat a healthy diet.

Record your training sessions below

Day	Time	Location	Activity	Signed
Mon 3rd	7am	Clifton Park	One mile run	AF
Tues 4th	4.30pm	College Gym	Training programme	AF
Wed 5th	6.00pm	Home	Sit ups / Press ups	AF
Thurs 6th	7am	Clifton Park	One mile run	AF
Fri 7th	4.30pm	College Gym	Training programme	AF
Sat 8th	9.00am	Clifton Park	One mile run	AF
Sun 9th	6.00pm	Home	Sit ups / Press ups	AF
Mon 10th	7am	Clifton Park	One mile run	AF
Tues 11th	4.30pm	College Gym	Training programme	AF
Wed 12th	6.00pm	Home	Sit ups / Press ups	AF
Thurs 13th	7am	Clifton Park	One mile run	AF
Fri 14th	4.30pm	College Gym	Training programme	AF
Sat 15th	10.00am	Clifton Park	One mile run	AF
Sun 16th	8.00pm	Home	Sit ups / Press ups	AF

Programme evaluation:

I redid the tests today and passed the press ups and sit ups, but I still didn't pass the shuttle run test. I'm not upset though as I improved my performance from last time by quite a lot so it proves the training programme is working. I just need to do it for a bit longer to get to the point where I can pass the shuttle run.

How would a fitness log like this help you improve your own fitness?

Activity: Keeping a research record

Research is an important skill when you are completing any qualification or even in any job you might do in the future. Your BTEC First contains a whole unit designed to help you research more effectively (Unit 19: Public Services Research). When you do any kind of project or assessment activity that requires you or your team to research information it is a good idea to keep a research record. There are several reasons to do this:

1 If you find a good information source it might be useful for other assignments, so you won't want to forget where you got it.

2 Your tutors may require you to complete a bibliography at the end of your work. This is an alphabetical list of all the resources you used to produce the work. You will have to do this on the BTEC Level 3 National in Public Services if you progress so it makes sense to start getting into practice now.

3 Listing the resources you have used helps your tutor know you have undertaken your research and may help you get a higher grade.

Recording your research activities:

There are several things you will need to note when recording your research:

- name of the author
- title of the resource
- when it was found
- where it was found
- summary of its information
- useful for any other assignment?
- other comments.

You could write this down on a piece of paper, but it makes more sense to put the information into a log that you keep in a ringbinder. That way all your research information is kept in the same place and you are less likely to lose it.

Conduct some research into the public service you are most interested in joining and complete the blank log below showing two sources of research.

Name:	
Unit:	
Assignment:	
Author:	When found:
Title:	Where found:
Summary of information	
Author:	When found:
Title:	Where found:
Summary of information	

Managing your information

Whether you've found lots of information or only a little, assessing what you have and using it wisely is very important. This section will help you avoid the main pitfalls.

Organising and selecting your information

Organising your information

The first step is to organise your information so that it's easy to use.

- Make sure your written notes are neat and have a clear heading – it's often useful to date them, too.
- Note useful pages in any books or magazines you have borrowed.
- Highlight relevant parts of any handouts or leaflets.
- Work out the results of any questionnaires you've used.

Selecting your information

Re-read the **assignment brief** or instructions you were given to remind yourself of the exact wording of the question(s) and divide your information into three groups:

1 Information that is totally relevant.

2 Information that is not as good, but could come in useful.

3 Information that doesn't match the questions or assignment brief very much but that you kept because you couldn't find anything better!

Check there are no obvious gaps in your information against the questions or assignment brief. If there are, make a note of them so that you know exactly what you still have to find. Although it's ideal to have everything you need before you start work, don't delay if you're short of time.

Putting your information in order

Putting your information in a logical order means you can find what you want easily. It will save you time in the long run. This is important if you have lots of information and will be doing the work over several sessions.

Activity: Organising your information

One of the most common methods of organising your ideas and information on your BTEC Level 2 First Diploma is in the form of a mind map. A mind map is a diagram which shows your research by using key words or phrases. It can jog your memory about different ideas or bits of research you have looked at and it can help you organise information ready for an assignment.

The mind map below shows information about uniformed public service recruitment.

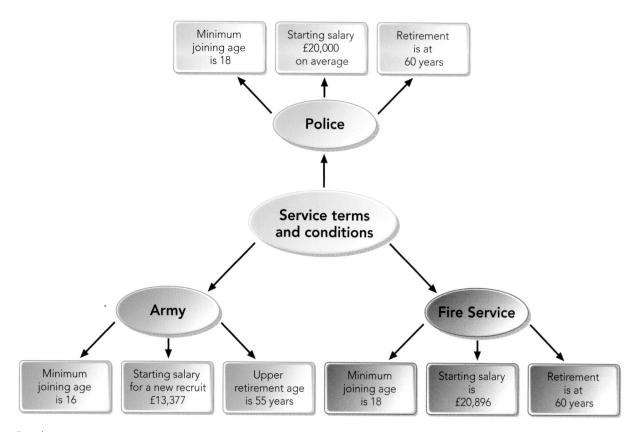

Produce your own mind map containing the same information for three non-uniformed public services.

Case study: Keeping a course file

'I've never been really organised, I tend to lose a lot of work and can never find anything when I need it. I knew I needed to be better at this when I started the BTEC First Diploma in Public Services as I would be studying seven units and I might get information that would be useful for more than one unit.

I needed a way of organising my information so that I had it to hand in every session and didn't lose it. I decided to buy a lever arch file and some divider cards and plastic wallets. I used the divider cards to split my folder up into seven sections, one for each unit and one for general information that I might need.

I made sure that at the end of each session I put any notes, assignment or research in a plastic wallet in the appropriate section of my file. That way I don't lose anything and it's always ready for me when I need to do some work on it.

The folder is always in my bag so I have it at home and at college. The hard part to begin with was always making sure I updated it at the end of every session but now I'm in the habit it's easy.'

Interpreting and presenting your information

The next stage is to use your information to prepare the document and/or oral presentation you have to give. There are four steps:

1 Understand what you're reading.

2 Interpret what you're reading.

3 Know the best form in which to produce the information, bearing in mind the purpose for which it is required.

4 Create the required document so that it's in a suitable layout with correct spelling and punctuation.

Understanding what you read

As a general rule, never use information that you don't understand. However, nobody understands complex or unfamiliar material the first time they read it, especially if they just scan through it quickly. Before you reject it, try this:

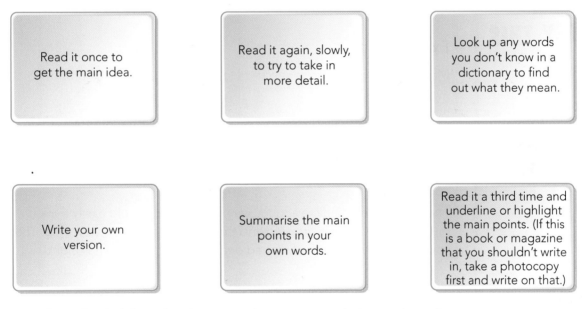

Read it once to get the main idea.

Read it again, slowly, to try to take in more detail.

Look up any words you don't know in a dictionary to find out what they mean.

Write your own version.

Summarise the main points in your own words.

Read it a third time and underline or highlight the main points. (If this is a book or magazine that you shouldn't write in, take a photocopy first and write on that.)

Special note: Show both the article and your own version to your tutor to check your understanding. This will help you identify any points you missed out and help you improve your skills of interpreting and summarising.

Understanding unfamiliar information

Interpreting what you read

Interpreting what you read is different from understanding it. This is because you can't always take it for granted that something you read means what it says. The writer may have had a very strong or biased opinion, or may have exaggerated for effect. This doesn't mean that you can't use the information.

BTEC FACT

In your assignments, it's better to separate opinions from facts. If you're quoting someone's views, make this clear. (See also page 61.)

Strong opinions and bias

People often have strong points of view about certain topics. This may be based on reliable facts, but not always! We can all jump to conclusions that may not be very logical, especially if we feel strongly about something.

Things aren't always what they seem to be. Are these boys fighting or are they having a good time?

Exaggeration

Many newspapers exaggerate facts to startle and attract their readers.

LOCAL FIRM DOUBLES STAFF IN TWO WEEKS!

This newspaper headline sounds very positive. You could easily think it means employment is growing and there are more jobs in your area. Then you read on, and find the firm had only four staff and now has eight!

Tables and graphs

You need to be able to interpret what the figures mean, especially when you look at differences between columns or rows. For example, your friend might have an impressive spreadsheet that lists his income and expenditure. In reality, it doesn't tell you much until you add the figures up and subtract one from the other. Only then can you say whether he is getting into debt. And even if he is, you need to see his budget over a few months, rather than just one which may be exceptional.

Choosing a format

You may have been given specific instructions about the format and layout of a document you have to produce, in which case life is easy as long as you follow them! If not, think carefully about the best way to set out your information so that it is clear.

Different formats	Example
text	when you write in paragraphs or prepare a report or summary
graphical	a diagram, graph or chart
pictorial	a drawing, photograph, cartoon or pictogram
tabular	numerical information in a table

The best method(s) will depend on the information you have, the source(s) of your material and the purpose of the document – a leaflet for schoolchildren needs graphics and pictures to make it lively, whereas a report to company shareholders would be mainly in text form with just one or two graphs.

Stating your sources

Whatever format you use, if you are including other people's views, comments or opinions, or copying a table or diagram from another publication, you must state the source by including the name of the author, publication or the web address. This can be in the text or as part of a list at the end. Failure to do this (so you are really pretending other people's work is your own) is known as **plagiarism**. It is a serious offence with penalties to match.

Text format

Creating written documents gets easier with practice. These points should help.

TOP TIPS

Don't just rely on your spellchecker. It won't find a word spelled wrongly that makes another valid word (eg from/form), so you must proofread everything. Remember to check whether it is set to American English or British English. There are some spelling differences.

Golden rules for written documents

1   Think about who will be reading it, then write in an appropriate language and style.

2   Ensure it is technically correct, ie no wrong spellings or bad punctuation.

3   Take time to make it look good, with clear headings, consistent spacing and plenty of white space.

4   Write in paragraphs, each with a different theme. Leave a line space between each one.

5   If you have a lot of separate points to mention, use bullets or numbered points. Numbered points show a certain order or quantity (step 1, step 2, etc). Use bullet points when there is no suggested order.

6   Only use words that you understand the meaning of, or it might look as if you don't know what you mean.

7   Structure your document so that it has a beginning, middle and end.

8   Prepare a draft and ask your tutor to confirm you are on the right track and are using your information in the best way.

Graphical format

Most people find graphics better than a long description for creating a quick picture in the viewer's mind. There are several types of graphical format, and you can easily produce any of these if you have good ICT skills.

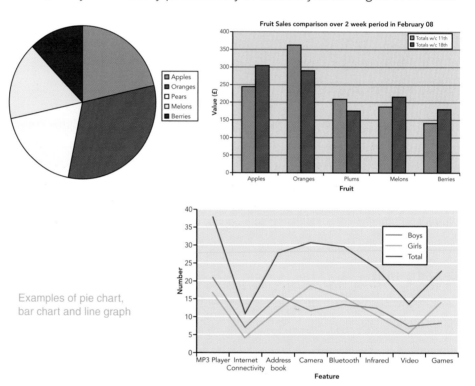

Examples of pie chart, bar chart and line graph

Pictorial format

Newspapers and magazines use pictures to illustrate situations and reduce the amount of words needed. It doesn't always have to be photographs though. For example, a new building may be sketched to show what it will look like.

A pictogram or pictograph is another type of pictorial format, such as charts which use the image of an object (fruit, coins, even pizzas) to represent data, such as the number eaten or amount spent.

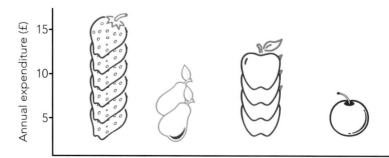

Tabular format

A table can be an easy way to communicate information. Imagine a retailer preparing information about the items in stock. Text would be difficult to understand and comparisons between stock levels and sales would be almost impossible to make. A table, however, would easily show the fastest-selling items.

Tables are also ideal if you are showing rankings – such as best-selling music or books.

Bestsellers list – September 2009

Position	Title	Author	Imprint	Publication
1 (New)	Lost Symbol,The	Brown, Dan	Bantam Press	15-Sep-2009
2 (1)	Complaints, The	Rankin, Ian	Orion	03-Sep-2009
3 (New)	Return Journey, The	Binchy, Maeve	Orion	17-Sep-2009
4 (7)	Sapphire	Price, Katie	Century	30-Jul-2009
5 (9)	Wolf Hall	Mantel, Hilary	Fourth Estate	30-Apr-2009
6 (3)	Week in December, A	Faulks, Sebastian	Hutchinson	03-Sep-2009
7 (2)	Alex Cross's Trial	Patterson, James	Century	10-Sep-2009
8 (4)	White Queen, The	Gregory, Philippa	Simon & Schuster Ltd	18-Aug-2009
9 (5)	Even Money	Francis, Dick & Francis, Felix	Michael Joseph	03-Sep-2009
10 (8)	206 Bones	Reichs, Kathy	William Heinemann	27-Aug-2009

National newspaper circulation – September 2009

	August 2009	August 2008	% change on last year	August 09 (without bulks)	March 2009 – August 2009	% change on last year
Sun	3,128,501	3,148,792	-0.64	3,128,501	3,052,480	-2.25
Daily Mail	2,171,686	2,258,843	-3.86	2,044,079	2,178,462	-4.45
Daily Mirror	1,324,883	1,455,270	-8.96	1,324,883	1,331,108	9.44
Daily Star	886,814	751,494	18.01	886,814	855,511	16.65
The Daily Telegraph	814,087	860,298	-5.37	722,644	807,328	-6.73
Daily Express	730,234	748,664	-2.46	730,234	727,824	-1.32
Times	576,185	612,779	-5.97	529,746	588,471	-4.63
Financial Times	395,845	417,570	-5.2	365,269	411,098	-6.7
Daily Record	347,302	390,197	-10.99	345,277	350,306	-10.59
Guardian	311,387	332,587	-6.37	311,387	332,790	-4.11
Independent	187,837	230,033	-18.34	148,551	198,445	-16.76

Activity: Choosing how to present information

During your time on the BTEC Level 2 First in Public Services you will have to produce a variety of different information in a range of formats. Some pieces of information may need to be presented in different ways so that your audience can understand them easily. Some of the different ways you could choose are:

1   written down in text like a report or a summary
2   graphical format where you produce your information in graphs such as bar charts or line graphs
3   pictorial format where you use images and pictures to show your information
4   tabular format where you draw a table to show your data.

Imagine you have collected the information listed in the table below. Which format might be most suitable for you to use when presenting the data? Complete the right-hand column of the table.

Type of information	Format
The results of a questionnaire about British involvement in Afghanistan	
The role of social services	
Your research on the numbers of ethnic minority employees in the local council	
Rank structures of several different public services	
A list of job roles you might find working in the National Health Service	

Making presentations

Presentations help you to learn communication skills.

Some people hate the idea of standing up to speak in front of an audience. This is quite normal, and you can use the extra energy from nerves to improve your performance.

Presentations aren't some form of torture devised by your tutor! They are included in your course because they help you learn many skills, such as speaking in public and preparing visual aids. They also help you practise working as a team member and give you a practical reason for researching information. And it can be far more enjoyable to talk about what you've found out rather than write about it!

There's a knack to preparing and giving a presentation so that you use your energies well, don't waste time, don't fall out with everyone around you and keep your stress levels as low as possible. Think about the task in three stages: preparation, organisation and delivery.

TOP TIPS

Keep visual aids simple but effective and check any handouts carefully before you make lots of copies.

Preparation

Start your initial preparations as soon as you can. Putting them off will only cause problems later. Discuss the task in your team so that everyone is clear about what has to be done and how long you have to do it in.

Divide any research fairly among the team, allowing for people's strengths and weaknesses. You'll also need to agree:

- which visual aids would be best
- which handouts you need and who should prepare them
- where and when the presentation will be held, and what you should wear
- what questions you might be asked, both individually and as a team, and how you should prepare for them.

Once you've decided all this, carry out the tasks you've been allocated to the best of your ability and by the deadline agreed.

Organisation

This is about the planning you need to do as a team so that everything will run smoothly on the day.

Delivery

Presenting and sharing work with other learners will be a regular activity on your BTEC First in Public Services. Whether you are delivering a PowerPoint presentation about a religion or secular belief you have researched or sharing a creative or therapeutic activity you have created.

Public services presentations

Presentations may form a large part of the work you complete on the BTEC First in Public Services. They are a key aspect of Unit 1: Public Services Skills, where you will examine methods of instruction in the public services, and Unit 19: Public Service Research, where you have to examine a variety of different presentation methods such as podcasts, PowerPoints and verbal presentations. They are also essential to get to grips with because the public services use them frequently to brief officers and the public. Being able to produce and deliver a good presentation will be a real advantage to you in your studies and professional life.

TOP TIPS

Never read from prepared prompt cards! Look at the audience when you're talking and smile occasionally. If you need to use prompt cards as a reminder, write clearly so that you need only glance at them.

TOP TIPS

Remember, the audience always makes allowances for some nerves!

Activity: Preparing, delivering and watching presentations

What are the key things you need to do when preparing, delivering and watching presentations? Complete the following worksheet to see how much you know. Have a look at the tips in the next case study to see how well you did.

Presentation	What you need to do		
Preparing	1	2	3
	4	5	6
Delivering	1	2	3
	4	5	6
Watching	1	2	3
	4	5	6

Case study: Presentations in pairs

Public Services learners at Wyndham School are in the process of completing their first assignment. They have been asked to research, prepare and deliver a ten-minute PowerPoint presentation on the skills and abilities required in two public services.

They are working in pairs to produce and deliver the assignment, and will have a booked appointment slot to deliver their work to learners in a lower year at school who are considering joining the public services course next year. The audience will be between 8 and 15 learners and the tutor for the unit.

They have been told to expect questions and comments from the tutor and the audience. This is the first large presentation the learners have done to an audience and they are nervous.

To help them, their tutor gives them a handout with some tips on how to make a good presentation and how to behave when observing others' presentations.

Tips for delivering a good presentation

- Speak clearly and look at the audience.
- Do not just read from notes.
- Your slides should contain bullet points and images, not a wall of text.
- Breathe deeply and speak slowly – most people talk too quickly when nervous.
- Make sure your body language is alert and attentive. Don't slouch or fidget.
- Make your slides interesting to look at with colour and images.
- Give your slides titles and check your spelling.
- Allow time for questions at the end.

Tips for watching other people's presentations

- Always have a notebook handy – the speaker may have used a really good source of information that you missed out.
- Note down some questions to ask.
- Be attentive. It's rude to do something else when you should be paying attention.
- Ensure any comments you make about the presentation are constructive and will help the group improve. After all, they may be watching you next.

Your assessments

The importance of assignments

All learners on BTEC First courses are assessed by means of **assignments**. Each one is designed to link to specific **learning outcomes** and **grading criteria**. At the end of the course, your assignment grades put together determine your overall grade.

To get the best grade you can, you need to know the golden rules that apply to all assignments, then how to interpret the specific instructions.

10 golden rules for assignments

1   Check that you understand the instructions.

2   Check whether you have to do all the work on your own, or if you will do some as a member of a group. If you work as a team, you need to identify which parts are your own contributions.

3   Always write down any verbal instructions you are given.

4   Check the final deadline and any penalties for not meeting it.

5   Make sure you know what to do if you have a serious personal problem, eg illness, and need an official extension.

6   Copying someone else's work (**plagiarism**) is a serious offence and is easy for experienced tutors to spot. It's never worth the risk.

7   Schedule enough time for finding out the information and doing initial planning.

8   Allow plenty of time between talking to your tutor about your plans, preparations and drafts and the final deadline.

9   Don't panic if the assignment seems long or complicated. Break it down into small, manageable chunks.

10   If you suddenly get stuck, ask your tutor to talk things through with you.

Case study: Assessment feedback

Shelley has just received feedback on a written assignment.

'I handed my first assignment in for the Public Services Skills unit two weeks ago and I got my feedback today. I had been a bit worried about it but I tried the best I could and I covered everything I could think of.

The assignment covered P1, M1 and D1 and I was hoping to have achieved all the criteria. The feedback sheet we got was attached to the front of the assignment and went into a lot of detail about the three criteria. I had passed P1 where I had to describe public service skills and M1 where I had to explain the importance of public service skills in at least two contrasting public services, but I hadn't passed D1 where I was supposed to evaluate the importance of public service skills in a specified public service.

The feedback was really helpful and it said that I hadn't really evaluated the importance of public service skills and I hadn't related what I'd written to a particular public service. Looking at the work with the feedback I can see the tutor was right. I hadn't really weighed up how important public service skills are and my comments were really general and didn't related to a specific public service at all. The feedback also said that I could add the additional work to achieve the D1 if I want to. I think this is really good of the tutor and I'll be submitting it with the extra work by the end of the week.

I learned it's really important to double-check your work before you hand it in and even more important to read the feedback you get so you can improve your work either this time or the next.'

Interpreting the instructions

Most assignments start with a **command word** – describe, explain, evaluate, etc. These words relate to how complex the answer should be.

Command words

Learners often don't do their best because they read the command words but don't understand exactly what they have to do. These tables show you what is required for each grade when you see a particular command word.

Command words and obtaining a pass

Complete ...	Complete a form, diagram or drawing.
Demonstrate ...	Show that you can do a particular activity.
Describe ...	Give a clear, straightforward description that includes all the main points.
Identify ...	Give all the basic facts relating to a certain topic.
List ...	Write a list of the main items (not sentences).
Name ...	State the proper terms related to a drawing or diagram.
Outline ...	Give all the main points, but without going into too much detail.
State ...	Point out or list the main features.

Examples:

- **List** the main features on your mobile phone.
- **Describe** the best way to greet a customer.
- **Outline** the procedures you follow to keep your computer system secure.

Command words and obtaining a merit

Analyse …	Identify the factors that apply, and state how these are linked and how each of them relates to the topic.
Comment on …	Give your own opinions or views.
Compare … **Contrast …**	Identify the main factors relating to two or more items and point out the similarities and differences.
Competently use …	Take full account of information and feedback you have obtained to review or improve an activity.
Demonstrate …	Prove you can carry out a more complex activity.
Describe …	Give a full description including details of all the relevant features.
Explain …	Give logical reasons to support your views.
Justify …	Give reasons for the points you are making so that the reader knows what you're thinking.
Suggest …	Give your own ideas or thoughts.

Examples:

- **Explain** why mobile phones are so popular.
- **Describe** the needs of four different types of customers.
- **Suggest** the type of procedures your employer would need to introduce to keep the IT system secure.

Command words and obtaining a distinction

Analyse …	Identify several relevant factors, show how they are linked, and explain the importance of each.
Compare … **Contrast …**	Identify the main factors in two or more situations, then explain the similarities and differences, and in some cases say which is best and why.
Demonstrate …	Prove that you can carry out a complex activity taking into account information you have obtained or received to adapt your original idea.
Describe …	Give a comprehensive description which tells a story to the reader and shows that you can apply your knowledge and information correctly.
Evaluate …	Bring together all your information and make a judgement on the importance or success of something.
Explain …	Provide full details and reasons to support the arguments you are making.
Justify …	Give full reasons or evidence to support your opinion.
Recommend …	Weigh up all the evidence to come to a conclusion, with reasons, about what would be best.

Examples:

- **Evaluate** the features and performance of your mobile phone.
- **Analyse** the role of customer service in contributing to an organisation's success.
- **Justify** the main features on the website of a large, successful organisation of your choice.

> **TRY THIS**
>
> Check the command word you are likely to see for each of your units in the **grading grid** in advance. This tells you the **grading criteria** for the unit so that you know the evidence you will have to present.

> **TOP TIPS**
>
> Think of assignments as an opportunity to demonstrate what you've learned and to get useful feedback on your work.

Activity: Pass, merit or distinction?

Students at Ironside College are completing an assignment for the unit Public Service Skills. They have been asked to produce work on the use of interpersonal skills in the public services.

The **pass** criterion requires students to:
○ Report on the effectiveness of various methods of interpersonal communication skills.

The **merit** criterion asks them to:
○ Explain the application of interpersonal communication skills in a given public service.

To achieve the **distinction** criterion they must:
○ Evaluate the effective use of interpersonal communication skills in a given public service.

Jamille provides a brief description of the effectiveness of various methods of interpersonal communication.

Sean explains in detail the effectiveness of a range of methods of interpersonal communication and explains how these skills could be applied in the Prison Service.

Daisy provides a detailed explanation of the effectiveness of various methods of interpersonal communication and clearly demonstrates how these skills could be used when working in the education service as a teacher. She also evaluates the use of interpersonal skills in the education service by highlighting how they help teachers do their jobs and the consequences to the teachers' job performance if they are not using effective interpersonal communication.

a) Who do you think has done enough to achieve a distinction?

b) Who would be given a merit?

c) Who would be marked at a pass?

Activity: Key assessment terms

When completing a BTEC Level 2 First in Public Services it is likely that you will come across the same words many times when doing your assignments. A good way to get higher grades is to know what these terms mean so you know exactly what work you need to produce. Some of the most common terms are listed below – what do you think they mean?

Assessment term	What does it mean?
List	
Describe	
Analyse	
Explain	
Demonstrate	
Evaluate	
Outline	
Identify	
Compare	
Justify	

Sample assignment

Note about assignments

All learners are different and will approach their assignment in different ways.
The sample assignment that follows shows how one learner answered a brief to achieve pass, merit and distinction level criteria. The learner work shows just one way in which grading criteria can be evidenced. There are no standard or set answers. If you produce the required evidence for each task then you will achieve the grading criteria covered by the assignment.

Front sheet

It is important to complete the front sheet of your assignment so that your tutor knows the work is yours and when you handed it in.

Time limits are set to help you manage your workload and it is important to meet them. Check your centre's policy on deadlines.

Ask your tutor if they will give you feedback on your work before you submit it, that way you can change anything that is wrong or add anything you have missed.

You must provide the specific evidence requested in the assignment. For public services this could take the form of presentations, reports, discussions, role plays, posters or practical tasks.

Learner name		Assessor name	
Munita Kassim		Ms Vivienne Thomas	
Date issued	**Completion date**	**Submitted on**	
1 December 2010	3 February 2011	1 February 2011	
Qualification		**Unit**	
BTEC Level 2 Diploma in Public Services		Unit 1: Public Service Skills	

Assignment title	Teambuilding and instruction

In this assessment you will have opportunities to provide evidence against the following criteria. Indicate the page numbers where the evidence can be found.

Criteria reference	To achieve the criteria the evidence must show that the student is able to:	Task no.	Page numbers
P3	Contribute to different teambuilding activities	1	Pages 1–5
P4	Explain the qualities of a good instructor and how they are used	2	Pages 7–8
M2	Demonstrate effective instruction skills	1 and 3	Pages 1–5

Learner declaration
I certify that the work submitted for this assignment is my own and research sources are fully acknowledged.
Learner signature: *Munita Kassim*   Date: *1 February 2011*

Pay close attention to the criteria you are asked to fulfil in your assignment and where you can find each task.

If you use other sources of work to help you make sure they are properly referenced. It is never acceptable to use work from other sources and claim it is yours. This is plagiarism and your centre will have a strict policy on this.

Assignment brief

'Participate' means you should join in with others to complete the task. You cannot sit on the sidelines and observe teambuilding activities: you must take part.

The scenario in your assignment is based on a realistic public service situation. It helps you relate the assignment tasks to the actual job of the services.

The title of your public services assignment will help you focus on the topic you are covering. Always keep it in mind.

'Contribute safely' means that you must be concerned with your own safety and the safety of others while completing the activities.

Unit title	Unit 1: Public Service Skills
Qualification	BTEC Level 2 Diploma in Public Services
Start date	1 December 2010
Deadline date	3 February 2011
Assessor	Ms Vivienne Thomas

| Assignment title | Teambuilding and instruction |

The purpose of this assignment is to:
Enable you to contribute to teambuilding activities and explore the qualities and purpose of good instructional techniques.

Scenario
You have joined a branch of the armed services cadets. They require you to be a good team member and also a good instructor. They have asked you to take part in activities in the course of which you will have opportunity to demonstrate both to their satisfaction.

Task 1
You are to participate in a number of practical teambuilding activities with your colleagues.

Select and safely contribute to five different teambuilding activities, recording your experiences and contributions in activity logs for each of the activities.

Submit the activity logs to your assessor. Your assessor will also provide an observation witness statement.

This provides evidence for P3

Task 2
Complete a written worksheet explaining the qualities of a good instructor and how they are used.

This provides evidence for P4

Task 3
In your activity logs for the group activities you chose for Task 1, record the ways in which you demonstrated effective instruction skills.

Submit the activity logs to your tutor when they are complete. Your tutor will need to sign them off to verify that they are accurate.

Your unit assessor will provide an observation witness statement to confirm that the grading criteria have been met for this task.

This provides evidence for M2

Sources of information

Textbooks
Institute of Management – *Personal Effectiveness and Career Development* (Hodder & Stoughton, 1999) ISBN 0340742941
Jay R – *How to Build a Great Team* (Prentice Hall, 2002) ISBN 0273663232
Murdock A – *Personal Effectiveness* (Butterworth-Heinemann, 2002) ISBN 0750656

This brief has been verified as being fit for purpose.			
Assessor	Ms Vivienne Thomas		
Signature	Vivienne Thomas	Date	19 November 2010
Internal verifier	Mr Ben Stead		
Signature	Ben Stead	Date	19 November 2010

Sample learner work

The learner has used her activity log to state clearly what teambuilding activity she is taking part in and how it was organised. This contributes to P3.

Task 1 (P3) and Task 3 (M2)

Activity log 1

Learner name	Munita Kassim
Qualification	BTEC Level 2 Diploma in Public Services
Unit number and title	Unit 1: Public Service Skills
Date	8 December 2010
Location	College football pitch

Activity description

Five-a-side football in mixed teams of males and females. Our class of 25 was split into five teams for a mini tournament.

How did I contribute?

We played four games in total. Our team won three and lost one. Because we played four games, we all agreed that it would be best to move round the positions to make sure we all had a chance to play in different positions and contribute to the team in different ways. I played in goal, in defence and in attack. This also helped us support each other because when you have done each job in a team you know how difficult it is to do it right. I think this made us better than the team who stuck with the same positions, because they were criticising each other a lot, whereas we knew what the other people in our team had to do and we could support them.

I also took the warm-up and cool-down for my team and acted as captain for one of the matches.

Evidence towards P3

How did I demonstrate effective instruction skills?

I demonstrated effective instruction skills in the warm-up and cool-down sessions. I kept to my timings so that everyone was ready to play their next match on time. I gave clear instructions about what I wanted my team to do for their warm-up and cool-down and took part in the sessions with them. My tone and voice was clear and I instructed them with confidence.

Evidence towards M2

Learner name	Munita Kassim		
Learner signature	Munita Kassim	Date	8 December 2010
Assessor name	Ms Vivienne Thomas		
Assessor signature	Vivienne Thomas	Date	8 December 2010

This section clearly sets out how the learner contributed to the team activity and is part of her evidence for P3.

This section clearly outlines how Munita contributed to the safety of her team which is important for P3.

Activity log 2

Learner name	Munita Kassim
Qualification	BTEC Level 2 Diploma in Public Services
Unit number and title	Unit 1: Public Service Skills
Date	15 December 2010
Location	Dearnetown Urban Combat

Activity description

We went out to the local lazer tag centre to play some games of lazer tag. This involved being split into groups of 12 and trying to shoot an infra-red beam at the opposing team members' chests, heads or weapons while running around a simulated city landscape with lots of places to hide.

How did I contribute?

I contributed by being an active member of my team. I achieved the second highest score in Game 1 and the third highest in Game 2. I warned other team members when they were in danger of being tagged, so that they could take cover, and I helped with several ambushes of the opposing team. I also warned a couple of members of my team who were being really silly and compromising health and safety – I didn't want anyone to get hurt. I was team leader for one game as well. I had to work hard to pull the team together so we could win.

Evidence towards P3

How did I demonstrate effective instruction skills?

I was the team leader for Game 1. After the centre instructors had briefed everybody, it was my job to come up with a strategy for defeating the opposing team. I gave my team clear objectives for what we were going to do and where they needed to be positioned. I demonstrated some of the ambushes we were going to do when we had the opportunity for a quick look around the arena. I also gave clear instructions about health and safety. (The centre instructors had already done this, but it is really important so I reinforced what they had said.)

Evidence towards M2

Learner name	Munita Kassim			
Learner signature	*Munita Kassim*		Date	*15 December 2010*
Assessor name	Ms Vivienne Thomas			
Assessor signature	*Vivienne Thomas*		Date	*15 December 2010*

The learner's worksheets clearly show her course, unit, location and date. This is good organisation and will help her tutor monitor and assess her activities.

The learner's worksheet also highlights how she used instruction skills which will help her achieve M2.

The learner shows she can act as an instructor for a drill activity. This is evidence towards P3 and M2.

Activity log 3

Learner name	Munita Kassim
Qualification	BTEC Level 2 Diploma in Public Services
Unit number and title	Unit 1: Public Service Skills
Date	22 December 2010
Location	College Car Park

Activity description

For our drill activity we had to do basic marching and turning as a formation. All 25 of us were in the same unit and had to learn the same moves and then perform them for our assessor.

How did I contribute?

I have been an army cadet for the past two years so I know how to do drill quite well. There were four other cadets in my class as well. After the tutor had been through the basic moves with us, it was really clear that not everyone was good at drill or had done it before. The four of us who were cadets were put in charge of perfecting the class's drill parade. We were observed for one hour while we tried to get it right. It was really cold in the car park too! I was allocated the group who was having the most difficulty. I saw straightaway that the main problem was their difficulty telling left from right while under pressure, so I asked them to roll up their right sleeve in order for them to be able to tell which was right and left more easily. It really improved after that. I was also part of the drill parade myself and my own moves had to coordinate with the rest of the squad.

Evidence towards P3

How did I demonstrate effective instruction skills?

As a cadet who knows drill well I was allocated the less able group to instruct. I demonstrated effective instruction by first watching where they were going wrong and then providing them with a way to overcome the problem. I demonstrated all the key moves lots of times until they could be copied. I used a clear tone of voice and a friendly manner – drill can be hard to learn when someone is shouting at you and you feel really under pressure. I was also interested in doing something different like drill as part of a taught session and I hope I communicated this to the team I was instructing.

Evidence towards M2

Learner name	Munita Kassim		
Learner signature	Munita Kassim	Date	22 December 2010
Assessor name	Ms Vivienne Thomas		
Assessor signature	Vivienne Thomas	Date	22 December 2010

Signing and dating worksheets will help you keep track of what has been completed and when.

Activity log 4

Learner name	Munita Kassim
Qualification	BTEC Level 2 First Diploma in Public Services
Unit number and title	Unit 1: Public Service Skills
Date	5 January 2011
Location	Field near college

Activity description

For our blindfold tent erection activity we worked in groups of seven, with one team leader who was not blindfolded and six of us who were blindfolded. The team leader had to get us to put the tent up correctly even though we couldn't see what we were doing.

How did I contribute?

I contributed by following the instructions of the team leader to the best of my ability and following all the health and safety guidelines we had been given. My main contribution was to sort out the shock cord on the tent poles when it twisted or came out of position. I had to make sure that the cord went into the tent pole sleeves correctly. I worked as part of a team to complete the task and although the tent looked a bit wobbly when we took the blindfolds off, we managed to put it up.

Evidence towards P3

How did I demonstrate effective instruction skills?

I didn't do any instruction on this task, which was the responsibility of the team leader.

Evidence towards M2

Learner name	Munita Kassim		
Learner signature	Munita Kassim	Date	5 January 2011
Assessor name	Ms Vivienne Thomas		
Assessor signature	Vivienne Thomas	Date	5 January 2011

Activity log 5

Learner name	Munita Kassim
Qualification	BTEC Level 2 First Diploma in Public Services
Unit number and title	Unit 1: Public Service Skills
Date	12 January 2011
Location	Classroom and College Car Park

Activity description

For our charity service, our class was separated into five teams. Each team had to come up with a way of raising money for a local special care baby unit and then put its plan into practice. Our team decide to do a college car wash. We decided to wash cars in the car park for £3 per car.

How did I contribute?

I came up with a list of possible ideas and shared them with the group. Everyone had different ideas so we had to discuss them and decide which one to put into practice. I took part in the discussion about which idea would raise the most money and be the most straightforward to organise. Once our team had agreed on the car wash idea, I brought in the sponges and buckets from home, while other team members brought the cleaning stuff and overalls. I personally managed to wash seven cars on the morning of the event and as a whole we washed 25 cars and made £75 for the baby unit.

I really liked this activity – it was cold and wet but it felt really good to know we were doing something worthwhile. It's the main reason that I want to join the services.

Evidence towards P3

How did I demonstrate effective instruction skills?

I didn't do any instruction on this activity.

Evidence towards M2

Learner name	Munita Kassim		
Learner signature	Munita Kassim	Date	12 January 2011
Assessor name	Ms Vivienne Thomas		
Assessor signature	Vivienne Thomas	Date	12 January 2011

Observation record

Learner name	Munita Kassim
Qualification	BTEC Level 2 First Diploma in Public Services
Unit number and title	Unit 1: Public Service Skills

Description of activity undertaken (please be as specific as possible)

Task 1: The learner had to contribute to five teambuilding activities (P3).
Task 3: The learner had to demonstrate effective instruction skills (M2).

Assessment and grading criteria

P3: Contribute to different teambuilding activities.
M2: Demonstrate effective instruction skills.

How the activity meets the requirements of the assessment and grading criteria, including how and where the activity took place

For P3, the learner took an active and safe part in five different teambuilding activities. These were football, lazer tag, drill, blindfolded tent erection and a charity car wash. I was able to observe the active and safe contribution of this learner in all five activities and signed the activity log as evidence.

For M2, as part of three of the teambuilding tasks, the learner had the opportunity to demonstrate effective instruction skills and has provided commentary on her activity log as evidence. I was able to observe all three instruction opportunities and confirm they were effective attempts.

Assessor name	Ms Vivienne Thomas		
Assessor signature	Vivienne Thomas	Date	2 February 2011

The learner could add
an introduction before
this table to explain what
'instruction' is.

Task 2 (P4)

Explain the qualities of a good instructor and how they are used.

Qualities	Explanation and how used?
Confidence	Confidence is feeling sure of yourself. This is important for instructors because if you are going to instruct others, then you have to be sure that you can do the activity in the first place and that you have the confidence to pass on the skills. If you didn't have confidence it might be difficult to get a team of people, or even an individual, to listen to you and take notice of what you were trying to tell them. This might have really serious consequences if what you were telling them about or demonstrating was something like health and safety because someone might get hurt. A good instructor uses confidence in his or her tone of voice, body language and way of speaking. A good instructor can use his or her confidence to motivate others and help them achieve what it is they are supposed to be doing. An example of this might be a situation in which you were learning to canoe: if your instructor was confident, you might be more willing to try the activity because you would trust him and that would motivate you to try harder.
Manner	A good instructor has a professional manner and balances being formal with being approachable. It is about the way you come across to others. You might not get the best out of people if you frighten them or make them nervous. Equally if you are over-friendly they might not take you seriously. You can use your manner to good effect as an instructor by altering it to take account of the needs of the people you are instructing. If your group are messing about and not listening, then you might have to be really firm with them; if they are scared and nervous you might try to be friendlier in your manner to put them at ease. A good instructor adapts their approach to the group they are instructing.
Way of speaking	Your way of speaking is about how you use your voice to communicate with others while you are instructing them. Your voice should be clear and you should vary your tone so that people don't get bored listening to you. A good instructor will vary his or her way of speaking depending on the activity. If you are instructing a group, you might need to raise your voice to be heard, but if you are talking to one person you will need to speak more quietly. A good instructor gives really clear instructions so that they can be understood by the people they are dealing with.
Way of moving	Your way of moving is about your body language while you are instructing and sometimes it is about how you practically demonstrate things too. A good instructor is confident in his or her movement in order to inspire trust and confidence that they know what they are doing. When demonstrating, a good instructor's movements might be slower and more deliberate than normal, so that people can see correct techniques and can copy them more easily. They might also repeat movements over and over until the person they are instructing has got it right.
Appearance	Your appearance is important because it is the way you look to other people. A good instructor will look like a professional in their job – they will be smart, clean and have the right equipment. If you look scruffy people might think you don't know much and they might not pay you any attention. If you dress properly, then you show them that you look like you know what you are doing. This doesn't mean you wear a smart suit or anything, but what you wear has to be right for the instruction you are giving. For example, if you are demonstrating something like motor mechanics, you would wear overalls. Sports instructors would wear sports kit and drill instructors might wear boots and uniform.

The learner has looked
at all the key qualities of
a good instructor listed
in the content. This will
help her achieve P4.

Attitude	Your attitude is important because it is how your present yourself to other people. If an instructor has a bad attitude, he or she might not have any patience with people who are struggling to pick up a skill and might lose confidence and walk away. A bad attitude might also mean that an instructor says horrible things to their students or calls them stupid or something. A good instructor has a calm and patient attitude and is supportive of the people he or she is trying to teach even if they don't pick up the skills straightaway. A good instructor will always be approachable – you should be able to ask a question as many times as you need, or be shown how to do something again and again without the instructor minding.
Diligence	This is about paying proper attention to a task and giving it the time it deserves. A good instructor will be diligent with her students and make sure they get the proper time and attention to be able to do a task properly. This is really important if the task is dangerous because if the instructor isn't diligent with health and safety someone could get hurt. For example, a rifle instructor in the army who doesn't pay proper attention when training people in how to use and fire rifles could cause serious injury to her students.
Enthusiasm and interest in the subject	Enthusiasm for the subject you are instructing in is really important. If you are interested in what you are doing, others will pick up your interest and like it too. If an instructor doesn't like what they are doing, then people pick up on it and become bored and lose interest themselves. A good instructor shares his or her enthusiasm with students and motivates them to want to find out more and perfect their skills.

The learner could have considered adding a conclusion to sum up the table.

Sample assessor's comments

Learner feedback allows your tutor to see how you coped with the assignment.

The tutor clearly outlines what the learner did well. This will help her take the positive aspects of her work into future assignments.

Qualification	BTEC Level 2 First Diploma in Public Services	Year	2010–2011
Unit number and title	Unit 1: Public Service Skills	Learner name	Munita Kassim

Grading criteria	Achieved?
P3 Contribute to different teambuilding activities	Y
P4 Explain the qualities of a good instructor and how they are used	Y
M2 Demonstrate effective instruction skills	Y

Learner feedback

This was really good fun. I got to do lots of practical activities and had the opportunity to help others to learn as well. My favourite bit was the charity car wash because we raised money for a really good cause and I was proud of that. My worst bit was the worksheet because it took time to do the research and think about what good instructors do.

Assessor feedback

You have done a really good job here Munita. You took part in five activities safely and with a really good attitude, and in the course of three of those activities you demonstrated your instructional skills. These are really very good – I'm sure your cadet background helped you there! Your worksheet is completed to a good standard and clearly shows that you understand the qualities of a good instructor and how they are used. I am very pleased with this assignment. Well done!

Action plan

When you use any books or internet sites you should list them at the end of your work. This is called referencing. Try and do this for future assignments please, although with practical work I know that there isn't much to reference.

Assessor signature	Vivienne Thomas	Date	16 February 2011
Learner signature	Munita Kassim	Date	18 February 2011

The tutor has also pointed out where the learner can improve. In this case she could improve future work by referencing.

Coping with problems

Most learners sail through their BTEC First with no major problems. Unfortunately, not everyone is so lucky. Some may have personal difficulties or other issues that disrupt their work so they are late handing in their assignments. If this happens to you, it's vital to know what to do. This checklist should help.

Checklist for coping with problems

✔ Check that you know who to talk to.

✔ Don't sit on a problem and worry about it. Talk to someone promptly, in confidence. It's always easier to cope if you've shared it with someone.

✔ Most centres have professional counsellors you can talk to if you prefer. They won't repeat anything you say to them without your permission.

✔ If you've done something wrong or silly, people will respect you more if you are honest, admit where you went wrong and apologise promptly.

TOP TIPS

If you have a serious complaint or concern, talk to your chosen tutor first – for example if you believe an assignment grade is unfair. All centres have official procedures to cover important issues such as appeals about assignments and formal complaints but it's usually sensible to try to resolve a problem informally first.

Case study: Coping with problems

Sophie describes her experience of coping with problems during her course.

'I did really well in the first two terms of my BTEC Level 2 First Diploma in Public Services. My grades were high and I had already applied to join the BTEC Level 3 National Diploma the following year. The problems started for me over Easter as we were going into the third term.

My dad is registered disabled so he can't work. My mum has always been the breadwinner in the house and she has taken really good care of me and my younger brother, as well as looking after my dad. Over Easter the company she was working for went bankrupt and had to lay off all the staff. My mum was devastated as she'd been working there for over ten years. My mum and dad started arguing a lot because of the stress of it all.

I couldn't just let them take all the strain, so my brother and I decided to see if we could earn some money ourselves to bring into the house. My brother got a paper round which he could do before and after school and I was lucky enough to get a part-time job in a hair salon sweeping hair and making teas after college every day from 5 to 7 p.m.

It went OK for the first couple of weeks, but then I seemed to have less and less time to do my assignments and I was getting further and further behind. The hair salon started offering me weekend work as well and I felt I had to take it because we needed the money.

My course tutor had a talk with me about my college work and I just started crying because of the stress of it all. He was really great. He called my mum in for a chat and she was shocked because I'd tried to hide how much paid work I was doing so she wouldn't feel bad about taking the money. We both had a bit of a cry and then started to sort things out. I've cut my hours down to two evenings a week and my mum has now got a job in the same hair salon working on reception.

The one thing I would say to anyone in my position is, if you are struggling, tell someone. Talking about my problems saved my college course. It could do the same for you.'

Activity: Knowing where to get help

Knowing where to go if you have a problem is really important.

Find out who you would go to discuss the following problems or issues:

Issue or problem	Where would you go for help?
You don't understand why you have been given a low grade for an assignment.	
You have problems at home which are affecting your work.	
You are struggling with understanding your work.	
You are having problems with another learner who is bullying you.	
You have changed your mind about what you might want to do in your career.	

Skills building

To do your best in your assignments you need a number of skills, including:

- your **personal, learning and thinking skills**
- your **functional skills** of ICT, mathematics and English
- your proofreading and document-production skills.

Personal, learning and thinking skills (PLTS)

These are the skills, personal qualities and behaviour that you find in people who are effective and confident at work. These people enjoy carrying out a wide range of tasks, always try to do their best and work well alone or with others. They enjoy a challenge and use new experiences to learn and develop.

Activity: How good are your PLTS?

1 Do this quiz to help you identify areas for improvement.

a) I get on well with other people.

Always   **Usually**   **Seldom**   **Never**

b) I try to find out other people's suggestions for solving problems that puzzle me.

Always   **Usually**   **Seldom**   **Never**

c) I plan carefully to make sure I meet my deadlines.

Always   **Usually**   **Seldom**   **Never**

d) If someone is being difficult, I think carefully before making a response.

Always   **Usually**   **Seldom**   **Never**

e) I don't mind sharing my possessions or my time.

Always   **Usually**   **Seldom**   **Never**

f) I take account of other people's views and opinions.

Always   **Usually**   **Seldom**   **Never**

g) I enjoy thinking of new ways of doing things.

Always   **Usually**   **Seldom**   **Never**

h) I like creating new and different things.

Always   **Usually**   **Seldom**   **Never**

i) I enjoy planning and finding ways of solving problems.

Always   **Usually**   **Seldom**   **Never**

j) I enjoy getting feedback about my performance.

Always   Usually   Seldom   Never

k) I try to learn from constructive criticism so that I know what to improve.

Always   Usually   Seldom   Never

l) I enjoy new challenges.

Always   Usually   Seldom   Never

m) I am even-tempered.

Always   Usually   Seldom   Never

n) I am happy to make changes when necessary.

Always   Usually   Seldom   Never

o) I like helping other people.

Always   Usually   Seldom   Never

Score 3 points for each time you answered 'Always', 2 points for 'Usually', 1 point for 'Seldom' and 0 points for 'Never'. The higher your score, the higher your personal, learning and thinking skills.

2 How creative are you? Test yourself with this activity. Identify 50 different objects you could fit into a matchbox at the same time! As a start, three suitable items are a postage stamp, a grain of rice, a staple. Can you find 47 more?

BTEC FACTS

Your BTEC First qualification is at Level 2. Qualifications in functional skills start at Entry level and continue to Level 2. (You don't need to achieve functional skills to gain any BTEC qualification and the evidence from a BTEC assignment can't be used towards the assessment of functional skills.)

Functional skills

Functional skills are the practical skills you need to function confidently, effectively and independently at work, when studying and in everyday life. They focus on the following areas:

- Information and Communications Technology (ICT)
- Maths
- English.

You may already be familiar with functional skills. Your BTEC First tutors will give you more information about how you will continue to develop these skills on your new course.

ICT skills

These will relate directly to how much 'hands-on' practice you have had on IT equipment. You may be an experienced IT user and using word processing, spreadsheet and presentation software may be second nature. Searching for information online may be something you do every day – in between downloading music, buying or selling on eBay and updating your Facebook profile!

Or you may prefer to avoid computer contact as much as possible. If so, there are two things you need to do.

1 Use every opportunity to improve your ICT skills so that you can start to live in the 21st century!

2 Make life easier by improving your basic proofreading and document preparation skills.

Proofreading and document preparation skills

Being able to produce well-displayed work quickly will make your life a lot easier. On any course there will be at least one unit that requires you to use good document preparation skills.

> ### Tips to improve your document production skills
>
> ✔ If your keyboarding skills are poor, ask if there is a workshop you can join. Or your library or resource centre may have software you can use.
>
> ✔ Check that you know the format of documents you have to produce for assignments. It can help to have a 'model' version of each type in your folder for quick reference.
>
> ✔ Practise checking your work by reading word by word – and remember not to rely on spellcheckers.

Activity: How good are your ICT skills?

1a) Test your current ICT abilities by responding *honestly* to each of the following statements.

i) I can create a copy of my timetable using a word-processing or spreadsheet package.
   True   **False**

ii) I can devise and design a budget for myself for the next three months using a spreadsheet package.
   True   **False**

iii) I can email a friend who has just got broadband to say how to minimise the danger of computer viruses, what a podcast is and also explain the restrictions on music downloads.
   True   **False**

iv) I can use presentation software to prepare a presentation containing four or five slides on a topic of my choice.
   True   **False**

v) I can research online to compare the performance and prices of laptop computers and prepare an information sheet using word-processing software.
   True   **False**

vi) I can prepare a poster, with graphics, for my mother's friend, who is starting her own business preparing children's party food, and attach it to an email to her for approval.
   True   **False**

TRY THIS

Learning to touch type can save you hours of time. Go to page 96 to find out how to access a useful website where you can check your keyboarding skills.

TOP TIPS

Print your work on good paper and keep it flat so that it looks good when you hand it in.

1b) Select any one of the above to which you answered false and learn how to do it.

2 Compare the two tables below. The first is an original document; the second is a typed copy. Are they identical? Highlight any differences you find and check them with the key on page 95.

Name	Date	Time	Room
Abbott	16 July	9.30 am	214
Grey	10 August	10.15 am	160
Johnston	12 August	2.20 pm	208
Waverley	18 July	3.15 pm	180
Jackson	30 September	11.15 am	209
Gregory	31 August	4.20 pm	320
Marshall	10 September	9.30 am	170
Bradley	16 September	2.20 pm	210

Name	Date	Time	Room
Abbott	26 July	9.30 am	214
Gray	10 August	10.15 am	160
Johnson	12 August	2.20 pm	208
Waverley	18 July	3.15 am	180
Jackson	31 September	11.15 am	209
Gregory	31 August	4.20 pm	320
Marshall	10 September	9.30 pm	170
Bradley	16 August	2.20 pm	201

Maths or numeracy skills

Four easy ways to improve your numeracy skills

1 Work out simple calculations in your head, like adding up the prices of items you are buying. Then check if you are correct when you pay for them.

2 Set yourself numeracy problems based on your everyday life. For example, if you are on a journey that takes 35 minutes and you leave home at 11.10am, what time will you arrive? If you are travelling at 40 miles an hour, how long will it take you to go 10 miles?

3 Treat yourself to a maths training program.

4 Check out online sites to improve your skills. Go to page 96 to find out how to access a useful website.

TOP TIPS

Quickly test answers. For example, if fuel costs 85p a litre and someone is buying 15 litres, estimate this at £1 x 15 (£15) and the answer should be just below this. So if your answer came out at £140, you'd know you'd done something wrong!

Activity: How good are your maths skills?

Answer as many of the following questions as you can in 15 minutes. Check your answers with the key on page 95.

1 **a)** 12 + 28 = ?

     i) 30   ii) 34   iii) 38   iv) 40   v) 48

  b) 49 ÷ 7 = ?

     i) 6   ii) 7   iii) 8   iv) 9   v) 10

  c) ½ + 1¼ = ?

     i) ¾   ii) 1½   iii) 1¾   iv) 2¼   v) 3

  d) 4 × 12 = 8 × ?

     i) 5   ii) 6   iii) 7   iv) 8   v) 9

  e) 16.5 + 25.25 – ? = 13.25

     i) 28.5   ii) 31.25   iii) 34.5   iv) 41.65   v) 44

2 **a)** You buy four items at £1.99, two at 98p and three at £1.75. You hand over a £20 note. How much change will you get? _____

  b) What fraction of one litre is 250 ml? _____

  c) What percentage of £50 is £2.50? _____

  d) A designer travelling on business can claim 38.2p a mile in expenses. How much is she owed if she travels 625 miles? _____

  e) You are flying to New York in December. New York is five hours behind British time and the flight lasts eight hours. If you leave at 11.15 am, what time will you arrive? _____

  f) For your trip to the United States you need American dollars. You find that the exchange rate is $1.5 dollars.

     i) How many dollars will you receive if you exchange £500? _____

     ii) Last year your friend visited New York when the exchange rate was $1.8. She also exchanged £500. Did she receive more dollars than you or fewer – and by how much? _____

  g) A security guard and his dog patrol the perimeter fence of a warehouse each evening. The building is 480 metres long and 300 metres wide and the fence is 80 metres out from the building on all sides. If the guard and his dog patrol the fence three times a night, how far will they walk? _____

English skills

Your English skills affect your ability to understand what you read, prepare a written document, say what you mean and understand other people. Even if you're doing a practical subject, there will always be times when you need to leave someone a note, tell them about a phone call, read or listen to instructions – or write a letter for a job application!

BTEC FACTS

Reading, writing, speaking and listening are all part of the Functional English qualifications.

Six easy ways to improve your English skills

1 Read more. It increases the number of words you know and helps to make you familiar with correct spellings.

2 Look up words you don't understand in a dictionary and check their meaning. Then try to use them yourself to increase your vocabulary.

3 Do crosswords. These help increase your vocabulary and practise your spelling at the same time.

TOP TIPS

If someone you're talking to uses a word, phrase or abbreviation you don't know, ask them what it means.

4 You can use websites to help you get to grips with English vocabulary, grammar and punctuation. Go to page 96 to find out how to access a useful website.

5 Welcome opportunities to practise speaking in class, in discussion groups and during presentations – rather than avoiding them!

6 Test your ability to listen to someone else by seeing how much you can remember when they've finished speaking.

Activity: How good are your English skills?

1 In the table below are 'wrong' versions of words often spelled incorrectly. Write the correct spellings on the right. Check your list against the answers on page 95.

Incorrect spelling	Correct spelling
accomodation	
seperate	
definate	
payed	
desparate	
acceptible	
competant	
succesful	

2 Correct the error(s) in these sentences.

    a) The plug on the computer is lose.

    b) The car was stationery outside the house.

    c) Their going on they're holidays tomorrow.

    d) The principle of the college is John Smith.

    e) We are all going accept Tom.

3 Punctuate these sentences correctly.

    a) Toms train was late on Monday and Tuesday.

    b) She is going to France Belgium Spain and Italy in the summer.

    c) He comes from Leeds and says its great there.

4 Read the article on copyright.

Copyright

Anyone who uses a photocopier can break copyright law if they carry out unrestricted photocopying of certain documents. This is because The Copyright, Designs and Patents Act 1988 protects the creator of an original work against having it copied without permission.

Legally, every time anyone writes a book, composes a song, makes a film or creates any other type of artistic work, this work is treated as their property (or copyright). If anyone else wishes to make use of it, they must get permission to do so and, on occasions, pay a fee.

Licences can be obtained to allow educational establishments to photocopy limited numbers of some publications. In addition, copies of an original document can be made for certain specific purposes. These include research and private study. Under the Act, too, if an article is summarised and quoted by anyone, then the author and title of the original work must be acknowledged.

a) Test your ability to understand unfamiliar information by responding to the following statements with 'True' or 'False'.

i) Students and tutors in schools and colleges can copy anything they want.
True   False

ii) The law which covers copyright is The Copyright, Designs and Patents Act 1988.
True   False

iii) A student photocopying a document in the library must have a licence.
True   False

iv) Copyright only relates to books in the library.
True   False

v) If you quote a newspaper report in an assignment, you don't need to state the source.
True   False

vii) Anyone is allowed to photocopy a page of a book for research purposes.
True   False

b) Make a list of key points in the article, then write a brief summary in your own words.

5 Nikki has read a newspaper report that a horse racing in the Kentucky Derby had to be put down. The filly collapsed and the vet couldn't save her. Nikki says it's the third time in two years a racehorse has had to be put down in the US. As a horse lover she is convinced racing should be banned in Britain and the US. She argues that fox hunting was banned to protect foxes, and that racehorses are more important and more expensive than foxes. Darren disagrees. He says the law is not working, hardly anyone has been prosecuted and fox hunting is going on just like before. Debbie says that animals aren't important whilst there is famine in the world.

a) Do you think the three arguments are logical? See if you can spot the flaws and check your ideas with the suggestions on page 95.

b) Sporting activities and support for sporting teams often provoke strong opinions. For a sport or team of your choice, identify two opposing views that might be held. Then decide how you would give a balanced view. Test your ideas with a friend or family member.

Answers

Skills building answers

ICT activities

2 Differences between the two tables are highlighted in bold.

Name	Date	Time	Room
Abbott	**16** July	9.30 am	214
Grey	10 August	10.15 am	160
Johnston	12 August	2.20 pm	208
Waverley	18 July	3.15 **pm**	180
Jackson	**30** September	11.15 am	209
Gregory	31 August	4.20 pm	320
Marshall	10 September	9.30 **am**	170
Bradley	16 **September**	2.20 pm	**210**

Maths/numeracy activities

1 a) iv, b) ii, c) iii, d) ii, e) i

2 a) £4.83, b) ¼, c) 5%, d) £238.75, e) 2.15 pm, f) i) $750 ii) $150 dollars more, g) 6.6 km.

English activities

1 Spellings: accommodation, separate, definite, paid, desperate, acceptable, competent, successful

2 Errors:
   a) The plug on the computer is <u>loose</u>.
   b) The car was <u>stationary</u> outside the house.
   c) <u>They're</u> going on <u>their</u> holidays tomorrow.
   d) The <u>principal</u> of the college is John Smith.
   e) We are all going <u>except</u> Tom.

3 Punctuation:
   a) Tom's train was late on Monday and Tuesday.
   b) She is going to France, Belgium, Spain and Italy in the summer.
   c) He comes from Leeds and says it's great there.

4 a) i) False, ii) True, iii) False, iv) False, v) False, vi) False, vii) True

5 A logical argument would be that if racehorses are frequently injured in a particular race, eg one with difficult jumps, then it should not be held. It is not logical to compare racehorses with foxes. The value of the animal is irrelevant if you are assessing cruelty. Darren's argument is entirely different and unrelated to Nikki's. Whether or not fox hunting legislation is effective or not has no bearing on the danger (or otherwise) to racehorses. Finally, famine is a separate issue altogether. You cannot logically 'rank' problems in the world to find a top one and ignore the others until this is solved!

Accessing website links

Links to various websites are referred to throughout this BTEC Level 2 First Study Skills Guide. In order to ensure that these links are up-to-date, that they work and that the sites aren't inadvertently linked to any material that could be considered offensive, we have made the links available on our website: www.pearsonhotlinks.co.uk. When you visit the site search for either the title BTEC Level 2 First Study Skills Guide in Public Services or ISBN 9781846905711. From here you can gain access to the website links and information on how they can be used to help you with your studies.

Useful terms

Apprenticeships
Schemes that enable you to work and earn money at the same time as you gain further qualifications (an NVQ award and a technical certificate) and improve your functional skills. Apprentices learn work-based skills relevant to their job role and their chosen industry. See page 96 for how to access a useful website to find out more.

Assessment methods
Methods, such as practical tasks and assignments, which are used to check that your work demonstrates the learning and understanding you need to obtain the qualification.

Assessor
The tutor who marks or assesses your work.

Assignment
A complete task or mini-**project** set to meet specific grading criteria.

Assignment brief
The information and instructions related to a particular assignment.

BTEC Level 3 Nationals
Qualifications you can take when you have successfully achieved a Level 2 qualification, such as BTEC First. They are offered in a variety of subjects.

Credit value
The number of credits attached to your BTEC course. The credit value increases relative to the length of time you need to complete the course, from 15 credits for a BTEC Certificate, to 30 credits for a BTEC Extended Certificate and 60 credits for a BTEC Diploma.

Command word
The word in an assignment that tells you what you have to do to produce the type of answer that is required, eg 'list', 'describe', 'analyse'.

Educational Maintenance Award (EMA)
This is a means-tested award which provides eligible learners under 19, who are studying a full-time course at a centre, with a cash sum of money every week. See page 96 for how to access a useful website to find out more.

Functional skills
The practical skills that enable all learners to use and apply English, Maths and ICT both at work and in their everyday lives. They aren't compulsory to achieve on the course, but are of great use to you.

Grade
The rating of pass, merit or distinction that is given to an assignment you have completed, which identifies the standard you have achieved.

Grading criteria
The standard you have to demonstrate to obtain a particular grade in the unit. In other words, what you have to prove you can do.

Grading grid
The table in each unit of your BTEC qualification specification that sets out the grading criteria.

Indicative reading
Recommended books, magazines, journals and websites whose content is both suitable and relevant to the unit.

Induction
A short programme of events at the start of a course or work placement designed to give you essential information and introduce you to other people so that you can settle in easily.

Internal verification
The quality checks carried out by nominated tutors at all centres to ensure that all assignments are at the right level and cover appropriate learning outcomes. The checks also ensure that all **assessors** are marking work consistently and to the same standards.

Learning outcomes
The learning and skills you must demonstrate to show that you have learned a unit effectively.

Levels of study

The depth, breadth and complexity of knowledge, understanding and skills required to achieve a qualification determines its level. Level 2 is equivalent to GCSE level (grades A* to C). Level 3 equates to GCE A-level. As you successfully achieve one level, you can progress on to the next. BTEC qualifications are offered at Entry Level, then Levels 1, 2, 3, 4, 5, 6 and 7.

Mandatory units

On a BTEC Level 2 First course, these are the compulsory units that all learners must complete to gain the qualification.

Optional units

Units on your course from which you may be able to make a choice. They help you specialise your skills, knowledge and understanding and may help progression into work or further education.

Personal, learning and thinking skills (PLTS)

The skills and qualities that improve your ability to work independently and be more effective and confident at work. Opportunities for developing these are a feature of all BTEC First courses. They aren't compulsory to achieve on the course, but are of great use to you.

Plagiarism

Copying someone else's work or work from any other sources (eg the internet) and passing it off as your own. It is strictly forbidden on all courses.

Portfolio

A collection of work compiled by a learner – for an **assessor** – usually as evidence of learning.

Project

A comprehensive piece of work which normally involves original research and planning and investigation either by an individual or a team. The outcome will vary depending upon the type of project undertaken. For example, it may result in the organisation of a specific event, a demonstration of a skill, a presentation or a piece of writing.

Tutorial

An individual or small group meeting with your tutor at which you discuss the work you are currently doing and other more general course issues.

Unit content

Details about the topics covered by the unit and the knowledge and skills you need to complete it.

Work placement

Time spent on an employer's premises when you carry out work-based tasks as an employee and also learn about the enterprise to develop your skills and knowledge.

Work-related qualification

A qualification designed to help you to develop the knowledge and understanding you need for a particular area of work.